What Experts Are Saying About
Tailor Your Fiction Manuscript in 30 Days

Need to rework your book? Zoe M. McCarthy's step-by-step reference guide leads you through the process, helping you fight feeling over-whelmed and wrangle your manuscript into publishable shape in 30 days. *Tailor Your Manuscript* delivers a clear and comprehensive action plan.

> —**Elizabeth Spann Craig,** Twitteriffic owner, bestselling cozy mystery author of the Myrtle Clover Mysteries, the Southern Quilting Mysteries, and the Memphis Barbeque Mysteries, http://elizabethspanncraig.com/blog/

* * *

Zoe has developed a guiding resource for beginning writers. Her method is designed for brainstorming, shaping, and revising the early draft of a manuscript. General and specific tips are offered for applying rules of writing to enhance one's story for a workable second draft. By exploring the plot line of *Love Comes Softly*, writers may examine their own work for stronger plot and characterization. Valuable tools are offered that enable the writer to develop a workable draft in only 30 days!

> —**Yvonne Lehman,** award-winning, best-selling author of 48 novels

* * *

Tailor Your Fiction Manuscript in 30 Days is chock-full of practical techniques. Numerous examples clarify problem areas and provide workable solutions. The action steps and blah busters McCarthy suggests will help you improve every sentence, every paragraph of your novel. If you follow her advice and implement her strategies, a publisher will be much more likely to issue you a contract.

> —**Denise K. Loock,** freelance editor, lightingeditingservices.com

A concise, detailed, step by s

— **Jamie West,** editor co

D1241841

Zoe's writing blog has always intrigued me. As a high school English teacher, I can attest that her tips on good grammar and her hints for excellent sentence and paragraph structure are spot on. But as an author, I also appreciate her ever-present advice that excellent skills are not enough: you must tell a good story, too. This book clearly shows how to do it all.

—**Tanya Hanson**, "Writing the Trails to Tenderness," author of *Christmas Lights*, *Outlaw Heart*, Hearts Crossing Ranch series, and coming in 2019, *Tainted Lady*, *Heart of Hope*, and *Angel Heart*. www.tanyahanson.com

* * *

McCarthy crafted an amazing self-help book that will strengthen any writer, whether new or seasoned, with guidance and self-evaluation tools.

—**Erin Unger**, author of *Practicing Murder*, releasing in 2019

Dana,

May you be blessed with wonderful writing.

Zoe M McCarthy

Tailor Your Fiction Manuscript

in 30 Days

Zoe M. McCarthy

SONFIRE MEDIA
A PUBLISHING COMPANY
GALAX, VIRGINIA

Tailor Your Fiction Manuscript in 30 Days

Published by Sonfire Media, LLC
PO BOX 6
Galax, VA 24333 USA

Scripture taken from THE HOLY BIBLE, NEW INTERNATIONAL VERSION® NIV®. Copyright © 1973, 1978, 1984, 2011 by Biblica, Inc.®. Used by permission. All rights reserved worldwide.

Cover and interior book design by Larry W. VanHoose

ISBN No. 978-0-9891064-9-8

Dedication

To my friend and editor, Vie Herlocker.

God capitalized all the letters in the trait
ENCOURAGER
when he wrote out the specs for you.

Acknowledgments

A book based on blog posts has a chance for success only if subscribers and commenters have found the content helpful. Thank you to all my blog's regular readers and readers who write comments that express how a post has helped them.

I wouldn't have taken on this project if Joyce Hart and Vie Herlocker hadn't pushed me to corral my posts on writing into a meaningful resource. Thank you for believing I could accomplish the monster project.

Attending to seven books in different stages of completion threatens a writer's sanity. John, you went beyond a husband who helps his wife's publishing career by taking care of the housework. You became my writing career partner and took over the accounting, marketing and promotion, and other tasks. I love you.

Thank you to freelance editor Denise Loock, who graciously provided edits to my publisher. I trust your advice and appreciate you.

When I opened the email with my cover attachment, it was like a great birthday surprise. As my editor said, "The tape measure is so symbolic of getting your manuscript to measure up to publishing standards!" Thanks to Larry VanHoose for an awesome cover.

And to my heavenly Co-Editor, I praise You and thank You, Lord.

Contents

How to Use and Benefit Most
from the 30-Day Revising Process

The revising method in *Tailor Your Fiction Manuscript in 30 Days* works for any fiction genre. It's designed for the writer who has at least a draft of a completed manuscript. The goal is to shape a not-yet-submitted, rejected, or self-published manuscript with low ratings into a book that shines. The method can also be a guiding resource for writers starting a manuscript.

Once you have tailored your manuscript, it may be ready for you to query an agent or an editor. However, no matter how proficient a writer is in the craft, he'll miss things other readers will see. Most authors have critique partners look at their chapters during the writing process. Many recruit nonprofessional beta readers to read their completed and tailored manuscript to find editing and story problems they missed. Also, many accomplished authors who have addressed all the subjects covered in *Tailor Your Fiction Manuscript in 30 Days* will hire a professional editor.

If you choose to hire an editor once you've tailored your manuscript, the good news is the editor will have less to work on because you've fixed most of your manuscript's problems. Your work will reduce the cost.

You and your manuscript are unique. You are accomplished in some areas of writing and less proficient in other areas. I assume you'll spend little time on some topics and longer on others. The number of days I allotted to each chapter considers this. Don't get discouraged if you get behind. You'll get back on track in a later section.

During Days 1-4, you'll address high-level plot and character problems. You'll be asked to answer "☐ yes ☐ no" questions. The purpose of these questions is to help you identify where your story has problems. Answer the questions as truthfully as you can. The quality of your manuscript depends on your honest perceptions.

This icon will be present at the beginning of each new editing day.

After short learning sessions, you'll complete ACTION tasks, signified by this icon. Sometimes, I'll advise you to postpone working on your manuscript until several ACTION items are completed. This is so you'll have enough important information to make the work on your manuscript valuable and efficient. A word-processing document or notebook will come in handy to record your ACTION answers. These answers will supply what you'll need as you work on your manuscript. Also to help you, examples are included in the learning sessions, or they accompany ACTION tasks.

Starting on Day 5, you'll work revisions on a SAMPLE. Your SAMPLE is the first forty-five double-spaced pages of your manuscript or 12,000 words. You'll revise this limited SAMPLE as you learn the principles, techniques, tips, and suggestions in the fourteen days from Day 5 through Day 18. On Day 19, you'll work on your ending. After Day 19, you'll have completed an edit of your SAMPLE pages, and you'll be prepared to edit the remaining portion of your manuscript during Days 20-30. To aid you with this editing task, I provide a comprehensive checklist that you'll customize for your personal needs.

BLaH
BUStER

Some of the tips and suggestions are called BLAH BUSTERS. These are designed to make your story stand out. Think of readers invited to dinner where three plastic tables, one for each course, sport paper plates and plastic cups and utensils. The three tables are like three story acts, and the tableware contains other elements of a novel. All functional. But don't you want to invite your readers to a table with a tablecloth, a centerpiece, china plates, and flatware? Look for this icon and be prepared to add bling to your story.

RESOURCES

At the end of each chapter, I suggest at least one resource that has helped me and contains a topic pertinent to a focus we cover in that chapter in *Tailor Your Fiction Manuscript in 30 Days*.

High-Level Perspective
Days 1 - 7

Send Your Characters on a Journey

A story is not a series of unconnected events, interesting or not.
Your story must have a theme, a plot, and interesting characters.

Welcome to Day 1. Today, we'll look at the high-level elements of your story. I suggest you create a word-processing document or purchase a notebook to record your answers to ACTION exercises. Examples for this chapter come from the movie, *Love Comes Softly*, based on Janette Oke's novel by the same name. Often, even in a romance, one character's journey dominates the story. This is true for *Love Comes Softly*; therefore, we'll follow Marty's story in the examples.

You'll spend three days addressing problems you identify in your story's theme and plot. So, let's get started.

Theme

Why do we begin with your theme? You'll want to be ready to state your theme when you write a proposal, pitch to an editor, write a back-cover blurb, and have conversations with readers. Identifying and becoming comfortable with your theme will help you improve your story.

 ACTION

State your theme. (Don't worry if you can't. I'll give you ways to uncover your theme.)

Whether or not you had difficulty expressing your theme, let's test what you wrote.

 ACTION

First, jot down the main values your protagonist struggles with throughout your story.

> **Example:**
>
> Marty has traveled in a covered wagon from the East with her husband to find the perfect spread to raise a family on. Immediately after they stake their claim, her husband, Aaron, dies. A settler, Clark Davis, has lost his wife and proposes marriage in name only so he can provide a mother for his daughter, Missie. Marty wants only to go back East. Throughout the story, Marty struggles with grief, fear of the unknown, anything she can't control, and having a place to belong.

 ACTION

Next, recalling your protagonist's main struggles, peruse the list of short themes in the table at the end of this section. Which best describes what your protagonist grapples with in your story?

> **Example:**
>
> For Marty's story, I marked Abandonment, Loss/Grief, Uncertainty, and Place to Belong. These all apply, but Marty's main struggle is with a Place to Belong. Arriving in the unknown West, she thinks she'll be fine as long as she's with her husband. When he dies, she wants to go back to familiar territory, refusing to accept there's no one to go back to in the East. She's sure she doesn't belong with strangers—a man who wants her to mother his child and his daughter who wants her to leave.

 ACTION

Now, expand on that theme. What does your story say about this short theme? Write it in the form of a general question, one that's universal for people.

Example:

What happens when circumstances leave a person with no place to call home?

 ACTION

Finally, turn your question into a statement that is specific to your protagonist.

Example:

A widow finds security and love in a place she can call home.

Congratulations. You have a theme to work from as you improve your story.

When you include your theme in your proposal you may want to accompany it with a guiding quote or Scripture from the Bible. For Marty's journey to a place to call home, the Scripture might be Haggai 2:9. ""And in this place I will grant peace,' delcares the Lord Almighty."

If your theme is different than what you first wrote down, keep the revised theme in mind as we move forward, and you evaluate your plot.

Themes

Abandonment	Civilization	Empowerment	Government
Abuse	Coming of Age	Emptiness	Greed
Acceptance	Commitment	Enemies	Growing Up
Addiction	Communication	Eternity	Guilt/Innocence
Alienation	Conspiracy	Exploration	Happiness/Joy
Ambition	Corruption	Failure	Hatred/Anger
American Dream	Courage	Fairness	Healing
Answers	Death	Faith	Heroism
Appearances	Deception	Fame	Honesty
Authority	Depression	Family	Honor
Betrayal	Discovery	Fear	Hope/Despair
Boundaries	Disgrace	Fortune	Identity
Breaking Away	Disillusionment	Freedom	Ignorance
Bullying	Displacement	Friendship	Individualism
Chaos/Order	Dreams/Dreamer	Forgiveness	Injustice
Choices	Duty	God's Call	Innocence
Circle of Life	Education	Good/Evil	Insecurity

Intolerance	Nationalism	Rebirth	Skill vs. Strength
Isolation	Nature's Fury	Recovering	Social Class
Jealousy	Patience	Regret	Spirituality
Judgment	Patriotism	Rejection	Survival
Knowledge	Peace	Relationships	Suspicion
Law/Crime	Peer Pressure	Religion	Teamwork
Lesson Learned	Perfection	Reputation	Technology
Letting Go	Persecution	Responsibility	Temptation
Loneliness	Perseverance	Reunion	Time Travel
Loss/Grief	Place to Belong	Revenge	Traditions
Lost Then Found	Possessions	Rivalry	Tragedy
Love	Poverty	Roles	Trust
Loyalty	Power	Running Away	Truth
Lust	Pride	Sacrifice	Uncertainty
Manipulation	Prejudice	Savagery	Values
Materialism	Privacy	Second Chances	Vanity
Maturity	Property	Secrecy	Vengeance
Mercy	Punishment	Self-centeredness	Violence
Mortality	Purpose	Self-improvement	Vulnerability
Obsession	Racism	Self-reliance	Wisdom
Opportunities	Reality	Separation	Work
Oppression	Rebellion	Simplicity	

Plot

The story's plot takes your protagonist on a physical, emotional, and spiritual journey.

Clichéd Plots

Over time, superb book plots become so familiar and repeated that they become tired, and readers and editors put them aside. However, if your story's plot happens to be one that has become clichéd, don't fret.

Ways to make a cliché fresh:

- Do the opposite of your initial plan.
- Avoid stereotypical characters.
- Combine your familiar plot with another clichéd plot.
- Add original subplots.

- Imagine what your reader expects and then do something different.

Examples of clichéd plots:

- A love triangle
- Events turn out to be a dream
- Plain woman gets a make over
- The chosen one
- Portals to other worlds
- Dragons at war with people
- Rags to riches
- Look-alikes switch places
- Bad conduct blamed on bad parents
- Distressed woman needs a man to save her
- Wild hero finds woman who can tame him
- Retired man is the only one that can do the job
- Accused is in the wrong place at the wrong time
- Locals don't like the new guy in town
- Woman needs a stand-in boyfriend (or vice versa)

Is your story's plot a cliché? ☐ yes ☐ no

 ACTION

Don't rewrite anything yet. As you work through the Hero's Journey below, keep in mind the suggestions for making your plot fresh.

The Hero's Journey

A three-act-structure device that will help you locate plot holes or a sagging middle in your story is Christopher Vogler's "The Stages of the Hero's Journey." Vogler's twelve stages are an amended version of

Joseph Campbell's *The Hero with a Thousand Faces*. Don't let the stage titles throw you off. The Hero's Journey works for any genre whether the protagonist is male or female.

For the remainder of Day 1, simply respond to the yes/no questions and the exercises based on the twelve stages of the Hero's Journey. Your answers will reveal where your story is solid and where it may need some revisions.

I suggest you don't revise your manuscript yet. After you have a better overall understanding of your story in Day 1, you'll have Day 2 and Day 3 to make any needed changes to your story.

One important point to keep in mind as you work on the Hero's Journey is that it creates a character arc. Characters need struggles so they can display their extraordinary qualities. Conflicts, disasters, and characters overcoming and learning from their predicaments are the elements that build the character arc. Protagonists should be able to do at least one thing physically, emotionally, or spiritually in the end that they weren't able to do in the beginning.

Characters who risk nothing on their journeys do not attract readers. Readers enjoy stories in which characters face and overcome problems similar to those they experience. For love stories, the hero and heroine must have struggles outside their romance.

My examples for each stage of the Hero's Journey continue to come from the movie, *Love Comes Softly*. Most important, don't become discouraged when you must check a *no* box to some of the questions. Your rewrites in these areas could turn a good story into a stunning tale. Let's begin.

ACT 1 - Separation

1. Ordinary World

In the Ordinary World, you introduce your protagonist in his typical life in a sympathetic way. The purpose of this stage isn't to bore the reader with detailed information or backstory, but to contrast the hero's normal life with the new life he will soon enter. You should at least hint at your protagonist's greatest fear and internal and external goals. You can show the protagonist's Ordinary World in a few initial sentences or in as much as a chapter.

Have you shown the reader the protagonist's Ordinary World in which he's unaware of, or has limited consciousness of, his underlying inner problem? ☐ yes ☐ no

 ACTION

Describe your protagonist's everyday life in a short paragraph.

Example:

Marty and Aaron Claridge, young and in love, travel west with a wagon train in search of a good tract of land.

We'll look at your characters more closely in Chapter 2. For now, have you introduced your protagonist in a way that the reader has enough sympathy for her to care about reading her story? ☐ yes ☐ no

 ACTION

Give one action that makes your protagonist sympathetic to the reader.

Example (sympathetic actions in italics):

After they leave the wagon train, Marty worries they've gone in the wrong direction, and sick of riding through dust, she provokes an argument. This, and the wagon loaded down with Marty's books, shows she's a headstrong woman. During their dispute, Aaron stands beside Marty. Mid-argument, both see below them the perfect spot near a river. *The camera zooms in on her fingers searching for his hand.* Their argument forgotten, they imagine where they'll build their cabin and barn. *Happy, Marty kisses Aaron and says, "We can do anything as long as we're together."*

Have you revealed or at least hinted at your protagonist's external and internal goals and her greatest fear? ☐ yes ☐ no

List your protagonist's external and internal goals. If your story is a romance or has two or more main characters, you'll need to do this exercise for each.

Examples:

Internal goal:

Marty has gone along with Aaron's dream to settle in the West, but she wants to be protected from the unfamiliar. She's brought along her connection to the East by insisting they haul all her books. She thinks she'll be all right as long as she and Aaron are together.

External goal:

Marty wants to spend her life and raise a family with the man she loves, making his dreams hers.

Review your theme and goals. Write your protagonist's greatest fear.

Example:

Marty fears being alone in unfamiliar surroundings. We're given hints of this when she says they can do anything as long as they're together and later when Aaron prepares to go after his runaway horse and she wants to go with him.

2. The Call to Adventure

An event occurs that triggers a strong reaction from the protagonist. This event happens close to, or is part of, the opening scene and is called the *inciting incident*. The inciting incident calls the character to step out of his normal world and into a new situation.

Does your story have a clear inciting incident, such as

- something good, unfortunate, or evil;
- an event as small as another character's comment or as big as a spaceship landing?

Or possibly

- a wrong committed,
- a problem surfacing,
- a challenge egging,
- an opportunity arising,
- an adventure calling?

Or something that

- rattles the protagonist's Ordinary World;
- causes imbalance, externally and/or internally;
- and forces him to realize something must change from his everyday life;
- that he must face the onset of changes?

And this urges him to

- take action,
- make choices,
- begin to transform,
- become aware of his underlying need for change,

and hints at what the whole story is about

- because without this incident the story would be an entirely different story? ☐ yes ☐ no

ACTION

Relate, improve, or create your inciting incident in a paragraph.

Example:

> While chasing a runaway horse, Aaron falls from his horse and dies (inciting incident). Widowed, Marty ignores settler Sarah, who tries to help her. She holes up in her covered wagon in grief and fear. Another settler, Clark Davis, approaches her and proposes marriage, because he can provide her a place to stay through the winter and she can provide his daughter, Missie, a mother. Marty must make the decision immediately, because the preacher leaves that day and won't be back until spring. Clark promises he'll pay Marty's passage east in the spring if that's her wish.

Does your inciting incident occur after the story opens? ☐ yes ☐ no

The event happening before the story opens can work, but it may be more powerful for the reader to go through the incident with the protagonist.

3. Refusal of the Call

Once the inciting incident occurs, your protagonist has received the call to change. At first, no matter how brief, the protagonist should resist the call.

In other words, does your protagonist

- refuse to change,
- fear facing the unknown,
- doubt taking action is the right thing to do,
- balk at the challenges that seem too great,
- believe she's not the person for the job,
- want to go but others counsel against it,
- voice reasons she can't go forward, or
- find the status quo more attractive? ☐ yes ☐ no

ACTION

In a paragraph, describe your protagonist's reluctance, resistance, or refusal to set off on the adventure.

Example:

Before exchanging marriage vows, numbed Marty observes nine-year-old Missie's angry outburst about gaining a new mother. Marty tells Sarah she doesn't think she can marry Clark; she just wants to go home. At this point, Marty believes the lie that going back East is the only solution for her physical and emotional salvation.

A beauty lies in your protagonist's resistance to take the challenge. It gives you the opportunity to show her flaws, fears, desires, and the lies she believes.

4. Meeting the Mentor

Your protagonist needs a mentor to help him move forward, someone or something that helps him overcome his fears, doubts, or reluctance and inspires or pushes him past the inciting incident into the adventure.

The mentor can be a

- friend,
- wise person,
- counselor,
- tempter,
- protagonist's belief system or guiding principles, or
- source of courage or wisdom from deep within the protagonist.

The mentor can

- offer wise advice,
- provide critical knowledge,

- teach a skill,
- train the protagonist for an assignment,
- supply equipment or weapons,
- assist the protagonist to overcome obstacles,
- help the protagonist change when nothing else works,
- inspire the protagonist when he's down,
- calm the protagonist's fears, or
- execute a tough-love shove to the protagonist.

Do you employ a mentor whether it's a person or a nudge from within the protagonist to move him forward? ☐ yes ☐ no

ACTION

Describe the assistance your mentor provides to the protagonist.

Example:

Sarah warns Marty she must find a place to stay for the winter. When red-eyed Marty says she just wants to go home, Sarah counsels that this isn't a time to be crying over wants; now it's about needs.

Your protagonist may realize immediately that he must face the call, or he may agonize with doubts for an entire scene. But he must eventually accept the call. Thus, your story may no longer need the mentor after the protagonist internalizes his choice to move forward.

5. Crossing the Threshold

As the protagonist takes action and launches in a new direction, she commits to leave her Ordinary World and enter an unknown situation or place—a Special World. There's no going back. In effect, she's choosing how she wants the story to end. The question is will she get what she now wants.

Crossing the threshold could entail

- leaving town,
- taking a new job,
- dealing with a new condition,
- seeking medical help,
- sacrificing something,
- helping or protecting another,
- retrieving something taken away,
- rectifying an event that didn't happen as expected,
- following the money,
- impersonating someone,
- meeting a deadline, or else,
- accepting a new family role or responsibility,
- making someone pay,
- ending a relationship,
- changing living arrangements,
- stepping in for someone,
- fighting a cause, or
- fixing a situation.

Does your protagonist take an action that commits her to the adventure? ☐ yes ☐ no

 ACTION

Write the action the protagonist performs that commits her to operate in her new situation.

Example:

Realizing she has no other options, Marty reluctantly marries Clark. Even so, she's determined to go back East in the spring.

ACT 2a – Descent

6. Tests, Allies, and Enemies

At first, the protagonist feels disoriented in the new world he's entered. Therefore, you must allow the protagonist and the reader time to marvel at, or storm over, the hero's new situation. The hero must learn to navigate and seek where he belongs in the Special World. He builds new personal relationships. Some of his new contacts are allies and others are enemies. Of course, the people in the Special World may eventually reverse their roles. In a romance, the hero may switch from an enemy to the heroine's love interest.

During this stage

- the hero experiments with what works and what doesn't in his new situation;
- he figures out who are his allies and his enemies and evaluates which teams to join;
- he may share his backstory with a new friend;
- he faces minor struggles and disappointments, which escalate into setbacks that would defeat a weaker person;
- he's cautious, and may also be confused, which causes him to make snap judgments about others or himself;
- he undergoes development of his character from these under-pressure challenges; and
- he draws the reader to vicariously bond to him with each new trial.

One caution: Make sure the tests and struggles in this stage leave room for bigger crises at the later Ordeal and Resurrection stages.

As your protagonist enters his new situation or Special World, does he sort out who his enemies and friends are? ☐ yes ☐ no

Does he undergo tests and struggles? ☐ yes ☐ no

 ACTION

List two trials your protagonist faces. Describe at least one ally and one enemy.

Examples:

Trial 1:

After the exchange of vows and now at Clark's cabin, Marty shuts herself up in the room she shares with Missie and cries and sleeps for days.

Trial 2:

Competent and hardworking Missie determines to show Marty she doesn't need Marty's schooling. Missie uses her farm knowledge to trick Marty and show how dumb city-girl Marty is.

Enemy:

Missie makes it clear to Marty she doesn't want or need a mother.

Ally 1:

Clark is sympathetic to Marty's grief and keeps things civil between Missie and Marty. He finds "incompetent" Marty endearing. He talks frustrated Marty out of leaving, assuring her that her grief makes her the right person to reach grieving Missie.

Ally 2:

Later, Marty observes how deeply Missie misses her mother. Then, Marty catches Missie admiring one of Marty's dresses. The tomboy angrily thinks Marty is spying on her. Marty secretly alters the dress to fit Missie, which reveals Marty's competency. Missy likes the dress, and they become allies.

7. Approaching the Inmost Cave

The hero has adjusted to his new situation and has built new friendships. Bruised but wiser from his trials, the hero's final destination is in sight. However, he's still fearful.

This is the final respite before the Ordeal. Characters bond as they prepare for a significant physical, emotional, spiritual, or romantic challenge they foresee.

In this stage, you deepen your characters and create suspense. For a greater impact during the Ordeal, remind the reader now how different the hero presents himself compared to who he really is.

During this preparation stage in the Special World, does your hero

- use lessons learned,
- reach a point where only deep courage can win,
- come to a place that hides the solution to the underlying problem,
- approach a spot where he'll fight a fear, gain a treasure, or save a loved one,
- try to understand those who stand in his way in achieving his goal,
- find he needs a mentor (an ally) to push him into the "cave,"
- choose between two worthy choices—between his external and internal goals, and/or
- surprise the reader with his new qualities? ☐ yes ☐ no

 ACTION

Describe how your protagonist prepares himself to face the upcoming Ordeal.

Example:

Clark discloses that he knows Marty is expecting and he's glad she'll have the baby to remind her of Aaron. His words touch Marty. Marty shows curiosity about Clark and his faith and looks less haggard. Although she still plans to travel East come spring after her baby is born, she settles into and enjoys her mother role to Missie. She instills in Missie her love for reading and teaches her to knit.

The headway Marty has gained in her grief and the friendships she's making with Clark and Missie caution Marty and Clark of an impending difficult separation in the spring. This fear is a tremor below the surface of their daily routines. Clark's longing gazes follow Marty, and she becomes reflectively quiet when the subject of leaving arises.

ACT 2b – Initiation

8. Ordeal, Death, and Rebirth

This is the midpoint of the story, where the tension ramps up again. The Ordeal is a tough test that threatens the protagonist's life, her sense of self, or her return to normalcy. The test causes the reader to think the protagonist has died or failed.

Has an internal or external crisis confronted your protagonist that

- forces her to face and battle her greatest fear or flaw, or
- causes the reader to fear for the heroine, that
- she might fail, give up, or die, but instead,
- she's reborn? ☐ yes ☐ no

Make sure the resolution is not a coincidence, such as the necessary expert or an angel appears at the right time. Readers expect clever solutions to characters' predicaments.

1. Has an internal or external crisis upset the lull in the story? ☐ yes ☐ no

2. Have you resolved the Ordeal with a solution other than a coincidence? ☐ yes ☐ no

 ACTION

Describe the Ordeal in three parts: the crisis, the "death," and the "rebirth."

Examples:

The crisis:

As the first flakes of a snowstorm fall, Marty spots Aaron's runaway horse, approaches it, drops to her knees at its feet, and grasps the frayed rope end. Her grief rushes back as strong as it was when Aaron died.

The death:

When Clark returns home, the snow is deep and the blizzard rages. Missie is frantic. Marty has not come home from her walk. By now, Marty may have frozen to death. Clark and Missie work together. Clark goes out in the blinding blizzard to find Marty. Missie fires a gun and pounds on a pot so Clark can hear in what direction the cabin lies.

The rebirth:

When Clark finds Marty, she's still kneeling at the feet of the horse, and is blanketed in snow. He carries Marty to the cabin. She and her unborn baby survive.

9. Seizing the Reward

This is a reward for facing the crisis and death. This could play out with the hero

- defeating an enemy,
- entering a new inner state,
- conquering fears,
- gaining new knowledge or a treasure,
- rescuing someone,
- acquiring inner personal growth,
- celebrating a victory,
- accepting consequences,
- receiving a weapon, token, a healing elixir, or new meaning to life,
- settling a conflict with someone,
- reconciling with someone, or
- letting go of anger, jealousy, or hatred.

Has your hero seized a reward after he's "reborn"? ☐ yes ☐ no

 ACTION

Describe the reward.

Example:

While Marty lies recovering from her time spent in the blizzard, she weakly voices to Clark what's bothered her all along. She feels Aaron abandoned her. Aaron should never have gone after the horse. The animal is happy, free, and alive, but Aaron is dead. Clark replies that if a horse runs off, a man goes after his horse. It's as simple as that. She finally accepts his reasoning. She's survived her grief.

ACT 3 – Return

10. The Road Back

This stage occurs about two-thirds of the way through the story. Sometimes a chase scene is associated with this period, in which the bad guys are after the protagonist's reward. In any case, the transformed protagonist finds the road back is bumpy.

The protagonist

- has nothing left to prove and, at first, he thinks he's won;
- may have a sense of acclaim, absolution, exoneration, or rest; so
- sets out for home or back to his Ordinary World with his treasure; then
- meets a new development or challenge;
- feels like things are falling apart and he may fail to attain his original goal;
- may believe someone will take away his treasure; but
- is driven to complete the adventure, to finish the job; and
- may choose between his desires and a noble cause— between a material goal and love.

One caution. The new development must not be as severe as the final crisis to which your story is building.

Does your story have a challenge rise up just when all seems well and the tribulations are over? ☐ yes ☐ no

 ACTION

Describe the brief lull and then the new development, challenge, or attack.

Example:

Marty, Clark, and Missie are gathered together for a happy Thanksgiving.

Missie questions Marty about her past Christmases. Marty's responses reveal she has no one to return to back East. But she brings up some distant aunt and indicates she still plans to leave.

They make Christmas presents for each other. As Marty and Missie work together, they bond into a mother-daughter-like relationship. Marty is now a competent prairie woman, but still struggles to accept Clark and Missie's faith.

Marty goes into labor and refuses to allow Clark to deliver the baby. When a huge pain comes, she reaches for Clark and begs for help.

After baby Aaron's birth, Marty's mentor, Sarah, relates that after she and Ben became widowed, they had to join forces out of pure need. Marty can't understand how they love each other so strongly now. Sarah explains that love isn't always fireworks but sometimes over time, love comes softly.

At this point, Marty's attitude changes toward Clark. After a moment of playfulness between them, Missie remarks that her father's laugh is back.

Then the barn catches fire. As Clark frees the animals, Marty cries out to God for Clark's safety. All Marty's possessions from the East are destroyed, but Clark is unharmed. Marty demands to know how Clark can believe in a God who allows his barn to burn down, his first wife to die, and Missie to be without her mother. Clark takes Marty to his bench overlooking the river, where he worships God. They sit and Clark likens God's care to his care for Missie. He says the truth of God's love is not that he allows bad things to happen but His promise that He'll be with people when they do. Clark asks if Marty would like to sit there awhile. She does.

11. Resurrection

This is the climax often called the *black moment*. In this journey stage, the largest crisis occurs, and the hero receives a chance to prove he's been truly transformed by his journey.

During this stage, the hero

- realizes what he has truly yearned for all along (more than his physical goals),
- faces his fears one more time,
- battles something that could cause consequences to what his Ordinary World will look like for him and others if he fails,
- makes a sacrifice at the threshold of death, then
- succeeds and emerges reborn on a higher, more complete level.

Does your story have a black moment event near the end of your story? ☐ yes ☐ no

If yes, have you resolved the crises without a coincidence? ☐ yes ☐ no

 ACTION

Describe the crisis surrounding the black moment event, and how you resolved it without a coincidence.

> **Example:**
>
> Spring arrives, and Marty has reconciled her grief and doesn't want to go back East, where she has no one. She hopes Clark loves her as much as she's grown to love him and Missie. In a note she sticks into his Bible, she writes, "The wagon train will be leaving soon, but I don't want to go. Ask me to stay. Love, Marty." When Missie moves the Bible in collecting Clark's laundry, the note falls out and slips partially under Clark's cot.
>
> When Clark doesn't ask Marty to stay, she's confused and crestfallen. The wagon train arrives. Clark, Marty, and Missie are disheartened as Marty packs. Clark struggles to keep his promise and not interfere with her wish to return to the East, but he asks her if she's sure. Without his love, she's sure.
>
> At the ticket office, each struggles to accept what they think the others wish. Marty tells Missie she loves her and clasps the locket her mother gave her around Missie's neck.
>
> In the women's wagon as the train departs, Marty hears a woman say that a woman must be either crazy or in love to want to stay out West. Marty, no longer

such a hardened woman, disagrees with the woman calling the West a godforsaken part of the country.

Clark and Missie return to their cabin, which lacks any sign of Marty or baby Aaron's existence. Desolate, Clark kneels at his cot to pray and spots the note. Elated, he rides off after the wagon train. He locates Marty and entreats her to stay. She says she must stay for the right reason. He tells her he loves her. She joyfully professes her own love.

12. Return with the Elixir

This is the final stage of the Hero's Journey. The protagonist has faced many struggles and "death," has become a new person, and has learned much. Now she returns to her Ordinary World with her treasure. Even if she doesn't accomplish her goal, she has succeeded and changed in some way. This stage wraps up the message and leaves the reader with a sense of the protagonist's completeness.

The protagonist

- has gained a new power, belief, or perspective that will benefit her Ordinary World;
- may be able to help the people she left behind if she physically journeyed away from home;
- may continue on her journey transforming others as she was transformed; or
- looks forward to (or accepts) a new life.

In this last journey stage, does your hero re-enter her Ordinary World transformed, bringing along some sort of treasure? ☐ yes ☐ no

 ACTION

Describe the hero's new Ordinary Life, his transformation, and his treasure.

Examples:

Clark brings Marty and baby Aaron back to the cabin and Missie. Missie's eyes widen and she whispers, "Mama," and runs into Marty's arms.

New Ordinary Life:

Marty is home.

Marty's transformation:

Life and love do not end upon the death of a loved one. Marty's now a real wife and mother to the living man and children who need her. She's in the place she belongs.

The treasure:

The home, husband, and family that she'd dreamed of before Aaron died.

Congratulations, you have completed Day 1!

Review and Revise

You'll use the exercises you completed during Day 1 in two ways. First, the no boxes you checked alert you to plot holes in your story, to areas where your story's pace has slowed, and to where your story needs meaningful conflicts, struggles, and disasters. Second, your ACTION answers can guide you to improve every stage of your Hero's Journey.

So, for the next two days, employ your work in DAY 1 to transform your story plot into one that takes your reader on an engaging journey with your protagonist. Don't worry about perfect paragraphs in any changes you make. You'll be working on those in later days.

RESOURCES

The Writer's Journey: Mythic Structures for Writers, 3rd Edition by Christopher Vogler

Will the Real Character Please Stand Out?

Main and secondary characters must resonate with readers.

Today, we'll evaluate your characters from a high-level view to see how well they jump off the page in a way that's identifiable to readers. Work through all the questions and ACTION exercises before rewriting areas in your manuscript. Instructions for Day 5 explain how to work on your manuscript from this chapter forward.

Main Characters

Unlikeable Protagonists

Readers want to root for heroes and heroines. A whiney, woe-is-me, or surly protagonist is difficult for readers to cheer for. A protagonist will have flaws, but readers must recognize that the person who lies beneath the flaws is one who has inherent goodness.

You have a problem if your protagonist

- bullies,
- patronizes,
- picks on weaker people,
- uses violence to get her way,
- gains pleasure from ruining others' lives,
- moans too much about hardships (lots of pity parties),
- gossips to hurt others, or
- lies constantly.

Is your protagonist a likeable person? Will readers want to root for your hero and heroine? ☐ yes ☐ no

 ACTION

For your hero and heroine, list and rank their flaws in intensity or harshness. Use the above problems to help you. Look at their actions and their thoughts, which show their motives and inner self. Then decide if any of the most intense or harsh flaws go deeper than failings and need to be removed.

> **Examples:**
>
> Marty is used to getting her way and stubborn. (These are flaws.)
>
> Although Marty dislikes Missie's mistreatment and stands up for herself, she remains the adult and is never mean to the child.
>
> Missie is stubborn, voices her anger, and is prepared to fight if pushed.
>
> Although grieving the loss of her mother and acting out against Marty's presence, Missie obeys her father and works hard. Her shenanigans never hurt Marty physically or are outside the normal range of a hurting child.
>
> Clark is bad at expressing his feelings. With two headstrong and warring females, Clark needs to be the kind, patient peacekeeper that he is, but he could have prevented crises if he'd told Marty how he felt. But that would have lessened the tension of the story.

Give your protagonists something they deeply care about and readers will forgive their blustery moments.

ACTION

List what your main characters care about.

Examples:

Marty cares about her husband and books that provide learning.

Clark cares about Missie and that she has a mother to help her grow into a fine young woman.

Missie cares about her lost mother and helping her father keep the farm going.

To change the unlikeable character into someone likeable, here's a technique to try. Rewrite her thoughts so she deliberately filters her desired response to one more acceptable. This will calm her sarcasm to sass. Remember, though, you're not only changing an unlikeable character's thoughts, you're changing her character.

Characters who have scenes in which only their thoughts are shared with the reader are called *Point-of-View Characters* (POVCs), i.e., the scenes are told from their *point of view* (POV). Protagonist POVCs must have thoughts that show they have flaws but underlying integrity. Non-protagonists who are POVCs should think thoughts that resonate with their underlying character, whether they're snarky or not. For example, an antagonist who's a POVC may have violent or patronizing thoughts.

Do your character's thoughts often sound abrasive? ☐ yes ☐ no

 ACTION

Find instances where your hero's and heroine's thoughts show their inner selves to be too uncompromising or prickly. Try changing their thoughts to what they would say aloud. If one's thoughts are still too caustic, rewrite them so they represent a person who has inherent goodness.

Examples:

Abrasive thought:

The flirt had better get out of her way before she knocked the girl's nose out the back of her head.

Filtered thought:

She clamped down on her bottom lip. How long could she resist getting in the flirt's face and giving her a piece of her mind?

The first thought is violent. In revamping this unlikeable character, I must show she's distraught but likeable. So adding the action of biting her lip shows she wants to control her anger. If the unlikeable character expressed herself aloud, she'd probably filter her actions and words to be more socially acceptable. Perhaps she'd just tell the flirt off. That's more acceptable for a likeable character's thoughts than the violent contemplations. And to give her likeability another boost, I'd have her resist telling the flirt off.

Plausibility

Characters must be interesting, memorable, and three-dimensional. But they must also be plausible. We've already listed your protagonists' goals and greatest fears in Chapter 1. Now let's look at their dreams, skills, and passions and how to make them believable.

Have you layered your hero's dreams, skills, and passions throughout your story, so they don't seem contrived when the plot suddenly needs them? (A sentence or two sprinkled once or twice earlier may be all that's necessary.) ☐ yes ☐ no

 ACTION

List your protagonists' dreams, passions, and skills that they refer to or use later in the story.

Example:

In the beginning of *Love Comes Softly,* Aaron mentions having to ditch boxes of food to counter the weight of Marty's books in the wagon. She responds that she wants to bring culture to the West. This sets up her expertise in teaching Missie and encouraging Missie's desire to read.

Have you done the research to understand your character's passions and the value she sees in things that mean nothing to you? (You may have to put aside your opinions to understand what she considers valuable.) ☐ yes ☐ no

 ACTION

List your characters' passions and identify those you don't understand well.

Example:

If you think watching football is a waste of time, ask sports lovers what makes them hurry home to watch a game. Employ their input in your football-loving character's thoughts/dialogue and actions.

Secondary Characters

Secondary characters are important and have specific tasks for your story. The mentor character we covered in Chapter 1 is a special secondary character. We'll talk about walk-on characters later.

The purposes of secondary characters are to

- flesh out a main character's identity,
- help move the story along, and
- give a main character someone to talk to, instead of the main character constantly reflecting internally.

If a secondary character doesn't fulfill these purposes, the character only distracts the reader from the hero or heroine's story and is unnecessary, no matter how charming he is. Cut the character or make him useful.

Sometimes one secondary character can undermine another.

Example:

A young widow has a special relationship with her mother-in-law. The mother-in-law is a nurturer and considers the widow her daughter. If the widow's mother is pulled into the story, even for a short-lived experience, the mother downplays the mother-in-law's purpose. The reader's emotions are split between two nurturers, watering down the reader's connection to either mother figure. Of the two, the widow's relationship with the mother-in-law is more important. She provides a reason for the widow to be in the presence of her new love interest, her brother-in-law.

Do all your secondary characters support main characters in significant ways? ☐ yes ☐ no

 ACTION

List your secondary characters (not walk-on characters) and ways each helps show the main character's identity, moves the story along, or allows the main character to share important information.

Examples:

Supports protagonist's identity:

In the beginning of *Love Comes Softly*, Sarah helps to bring out the depth of Marty's grief and how serious Marty's situation as a widow is in the West.

Moves the story along:

Sarah prods Marty to come to Aaron's funeral and to accept Clark's marriage offer. Without Sarah, it would have taken a long time for stubborn, headstrong Marty to do either.

Conversations reveal something about the protagonist:

Later in the story, Marty and Sarah discuss how a woman can love again, even a man she normally wouldn't have chosen. Without Sarah's input, Marty would have mulled a long time over such a concept.

Sarah never appears unless she helps Marty sort something out or moves the story along.

Walk-on Characters

Never go into detailed descriptions of characters who make a brief appearance in your story. When an author fleshes out a character, the reader expects the character to have continued importance to the story. They feel cheated when the character never reappears.

Have you kept descriptions of walk-on characters interesting but brief? ☐ yes ☐ no

Five Techniques to Characterize Walk-On Characters

Here are five techniques to characterize a walk-on character in a concise and easy way.

Watch as the five techniques in the five examples build a paragraph that reveals the situation and paints the character of a young woman's father:

1. Describe the character through his actions and dialogue.
   Dad burst through the diner door like an avalanche

2. Employ exaggeration
   carrying along a mountain of boulders.

3. Compare the character to a known quality or quantity.
   His Angry Bird face whipped left and right until he located us in the last booth.

4. Characterize the character with a word or phrase—instead of excess details.
   I grabbed Andy's hand beneath the table as Dad, the wart that no cutting, freezing, or caustic liquid could remove from my life, barreled toward us.

5. Give the character physical or psychological behavior that offers a sense of personality.
   He drew on his habitual sneer, displaying his left-side teeth from his

> canine to his molars—the sneer whose purpose I'd always thought was
> to release steam.

Here's the full paragraph:

> Dad burst through the diner door like an avalanche carrying along a mountain of
> boulders. His Angry Bird face whipped left and right until he located us in the last
> booth. I grabbed Andy's hand beneath the table as Dad, the wart that no cutting,
> freezing, or caustic liquid could remove from my life, barreled toward us. He
> drew on his habitual sneer, displaying his left-side teeth from his canine to his
> molars—the sneer whose purpose I'd always thought was to release steam.

The father's character enters this one scene to do his job. The paragraph gives us not only enough about him to see what kind of person he is, but it tells us something about the daughter's life with her father.

 ACTION

Choose a walk-on character and apply one or more of the above techniques to write a sentence or short paragraph that shows his character.

Round Out Flat Characters

Archetypes

Sometimes the hero and heroine or a main and a secondary character sound like each other in their thoughts, dialogue, actions, and values. Possibly the author is so focused on plot that she has overlaid herself onto several characters.

Do your characters come across as distinct, well-rounded personalities? ☐ yes ☐ no

Using *archetypes* is an easy way to assure your characters are unique from those surrounding them: protagonist, love interest, antagonist, mentor, sidekick, and other characters. Archetype is defined here as a type of person whose typical behaviors are the same as those of numerous others of the same type. At the end of this segment is a list of many archetypes.

Your characters should think, talk, act, and have the values of their archetypes. Giving each character a combination of two or three archetypes makes him more interesting.

 ACTION

For each character other than those with minor roles, list one to three archetypes the character embodies. Looking across your characters, compare their lists of archetypes and identify characters who are too similar to others.

Archetypes in *Love Comes Softly*

Marty	**Clark**	**Missie**	**Sarah**
Teacher	*Parent*	*Innocent*	*Survivor*
Dreamer	*Mediator*	*Loyalist*	*Messenger*
Skeptic	*Peacekeeper*	*Manipulator*	*Mother Figure*

Note that none of the characters in *Love Comes Softly* share an archetype.

Sample of Archetypes

Addict	Dreamer	Innocent	Loyalist
Analyst	Enabler	Introvert	Macho-man
Anti-hero	Explorer	Invalid	Manipulator
Artist	Feminist	Investigator	Martyr
Benefactor	Fool	Jester	Masochist
Betrayer	Go-getter	Know-it-all	Masquerader
Bully	Hero	Leader	Mediator
Corrupter	Heroine	Loner	Messenger
Coward	Imposter	Lover	Monster

Mother Figure	Rebel	Seductress	Trickster
Narcissist	Reformer	Show-off	Tyrant
Outlaw	Revolutionary	Skeptic	Victim
Parent	Rival	Slave	Villain
Peacemaker	Rogue	Spoilsport	Waif
Penitent	Rule-keeper	Superpower	Warrior
Perfectionist	Ruler	Survivor	Watcher
Pessimist	Sage	Teacher	Womanizer
Pleaser	Samaritan	Tempter	Youth
Predator	Scapegoat	Thief	
Psychopath	Scholar	Thrill-seeker	

Traits and Thoughts

Related to archetypes are character traits. Each POVC's thoughts are typically consistent with their character traits, such as bold, adventurous, easygoing, organized, thrifty, and analytical. Consider your characters' traits in writing their thoughts.

 ACTION

For each character, list traits she or he exhibits. Later, you'll consider these traits as you review your POVCs' thoughts.

Examples:

The following are the thoughts of people at the same party.

Diplomatic:

Jerry was drinking too much. Maybe if he asked the guy to look at his car's starter problem, he could draw him away from the booze.

Humble:

If only Erin would stop praising her for helping with the party. Lots of people helped.

Independent:

If John didn't stop instructing him, he'd forget the bungee jumping until John moved on to something else.

Introverted:

Man, it was crowded. Maybe he could slip out early. Uh oh. Chatty Pam spotted him. Time to visit the restroom.

Meticulous:

Utter chaos. She'd best tell everyone exactly what they were supposed to do in the game.

Innocent:

Why was Cassie upset? Surely, John danced with Lola just to be polite.

Ambitious:

Forget the chitchat. Anthony over there was racking up prizes. No way would he let Anthony get ahead of his count.

Patient:

That was the second time Anthony butted in line. Oh, well, if it was that important to the guy, let him.

Nurturing:

Poor Jill had goose bumps. She'd take a sweater to her when she finished copying her cherry pie recipe. Jill's nieces would love the dessert.

Honest:

Erin had reimbursed her too much for the shrimp. Hopefully she had enough cash in her purse to make it right.

More examples of traits to consider:

Charming, patriotic, professional, protective, traditional, and flirtatious.

Character's Backstory and Prologues

Include a *prologue* only if the reader needs to know some major event that happened long ago, which is a foundation for the present situation in Chapter 1. It should be an event that the author can't easily feed bits into the story.

Backstory is often important for stories that depend on the reader's empathy. If your manuscript is an action, superhero, or mystery, backstory may not be important to your plot. In any genre, experts recommend backstory be banned from the first chapter. Readers are usually anxious to get into the present story situation.

Backstory is always important for the author to know, but sometimes it doesn't add anything to the present story. In this case, use it to develop your character but leave it out of the story.

When backstory is revealed in later chapters, it should be fed into the story a little at a time. Another reason to sift in backstory is to allow it to unfold like a mystery. For example, a character, who has reached a critical decision-making moment in Act 2, finally shares with a secondary character his past event. This is an excellent technique to prevent a sagging middle.

Have you resisted dumping backstory into your first chapter? ☐ yes ☐ no

You can hint at backstory in the first chapter. Knowing the character's backstory, you can use it to show how she navigates her world. In the first chapter, you can allow your heroine to exhibit what her past has caused her to become. How her past has shaped her will show through her values, her attitude, and her desires. Depending on the nature of past events, you can show in the present how she handles feelings, such as shame, guilt, fear, courage, loss, or love. You might also show how she regards the future. Then when bits of backstory are offered, they will make sense.

 ACTION

Describe any event in your character's past that is important for the reader to learn. List traits a person with such a past would have developed. Hopefully they are the same as you listed in the previous ACTION exercise. Now, give three thoughts and three behaviors that person would exhibit.

Examples:

Past event:

Except for an unfamiliar aunt, Marty has no family left back East. All have died. This revelation occurs later in the story, and Marty is defensive in admitting it. Readers may be surprised at first, because after Aaron died, Marty had been so adamant about returning East. However, her hanging on to the East makes sense when it's seen as her security blanket, one she'll need as long as the unfamiliar West doesn't provide what she had with Aaron.

Traits:

Marty clings to her books, which represent the East. She also clings to Aaron. In her need to feel secure, she's become headstrong about her books and Aaron because they're all she has left.

Thoughts and behaviors:

In the movie's beginning, Marty has insisted that her books remain in the wagon, and because of them, Aaron has had to toss food bags to lighten the load. She indirectly voices her fear of being without family when she tells Aaron they can do anything as long as they're together. Again, just before Aaron rides off to find his horse and to his death, she doesn't want him to leave her behind alone. The subtext is, "I'll be all right as long as I have you."

 ACTION

Review the past event you described in the last ACTION exercise. If you included backstory in the first chapter, list what pieces of the backstory you could filter into the second or later chapters or reserve for Act 2 to give the story's middle a boost. Alternately, show the protagonist's behaviors that have emerged from her backstory in the first chapter, instead of telling her past.

Review and Revise

From this point forward, you'll apply your ACTION items to the first forty-five double-spaced pages of your manuscript or 12,000 words. This is your SAMPLE to work on as you learn the principles, techniques, tips, or suggestions in the next fourteen days. Not only will you complete the edit of your SAMPLE, you will be prepared, with the help of a checklist, to edit the remaining portion of your manuscript during Days 20-30. So, let's get started.

 ACTION

Review your no answers in Day 4 and use your ACTION answers to rewrite or improve your characters in your SAMPLE.

RESOURCES

The Negative Trait Thesaurus by Angela Ackerman & Becca Puglisi

The Positive Trait Thesaurus by Angela Ackerman & Becca Puglisi

The Emotional Wound Thesaurus by Angela Ackerman & Becca Puglisi

Stein on Writing: A Master Editor of Some of the Most Successful Writers of Our Century Shares His Craft Techniques and Strategies by Sol Stein

Plant Your Character (and Reader) in a Setting

*Choosing an unusual setting is not as important
as making the setting you choose come alive for the reader.*

Reveal your character's location by the second sentence if possible. Don't make the reader try to figure out where he is.

A story setting provides the environment in which your drama unfolds. It's more than the place(s) where the author sets characters. It's interactive—creating the mood, giving meaning to the plot, and strengthening the story's theme.

Elements of Setting

Here's a table that includes examples and shows how setting encompasses more than a place. Keep this table in mind as we work through this chapter.

Element	Example 1	Example 2	Example 3	Example 4
Locale	school	neighborhood	city	island
Weather	fog	snow	tsunami	sand storm
Atmosphere	lighting	humidity	clutter	noise
Props	candle	lei	bowie knife	vacuum cleaner
Era	Civil War	Roaring 20s	Ancient Greece	Information Age
Time	1942	summer	Christmas	February
Culture	social practices	laws	fads	morals & mores
Geography	mountains	plains	marshes	deserts
Plant/animal life	whales	palms	rice paddies	kangaroos
Population	dense	small town	military camp	deserted island
Manmade entities	ports	pyramids	museums	burial grounds
Agriculture	vineyard	ranch	crops	minerals
Ancestral heritage	tribe	cuisine	dialect	religions
Climate influences	ocean currents	notable winds	latitude	tropic
Fantasy/Sci-fi	portals	phenomena	future era	topography

Using analogies and the character's senses are good ways to build a vivid setting. The character should react to his surrounding according to his goals, attitudes, and history. For example, if a detective is searching an area where an armed criminal has just been spotted, he's not going to notice the loveliness of red tulips in flowerbeds. But he might observe the disturbed mulch surrounding the red tulips in the flower bed.

Avoid "clichéd" settings, such as the hero and heroine conversing while eating inside a restaurant.

Setting is important, but don't bore readers with details they can already picture. The only time to go into details is to slow the pace to build suspense. In the example below, see how the setting description slows down revealing the diamond thief.

Example:

"I know who took Aunt Mildred's diamonds." Courtney stood, skirted the brocade, pleated ottoman, and poured a glass of lemonade at the mahogany buffet. She turned to face the ladies straining toward her from their satin-covered armchairs and settees.

Ensuring the Setting Makes Sense

If your story is set in a real place:

1. Have you chosen a locality that fits the mood of your story? ☐ yes ☐ no

2. Have you included a well-known landmark? ☐ yes ☐ no

3. Have you assumed many readers are unfamiliar with the place? ☐ yes ☐ no

4. Have you avoided being derogatory about the city or town and entities within it? ☐ yes ☐ no

(▶) ACTION

Describe the mood of your story and the mood of the place(s) you've chosen for the setting. Most likely, a light and humorous story won't work well in a dreary or dangerous area.

(▶) ACTION

List any landmarks in your story's setting. Readers expect popular landmarks they've seen or heard about to receive at least a brief appearance in the story. On the other hand, pretend your reader knows nothing about the landmark or city. Sometimes writers give sketchy descriptions of places, believing everyone knows familiar settings as well as they do. Record details readers need to understand what the landmark is.

Example:

The Corcovado Christ in Rio De Janeiro, Brazil is a popular landmark. But it's not as well known as the Eiffel Tower. Therefore, a few words about its color, size, history, and where it stands would be helpful to many readers.

 ACTION

Recall opinions you've blatantly or suggestively given about your setting that might offend readers who live or enjoy visiting the place. I'm not referring to a character's opinion that fits his personality. Jack thinks Miami, Florida is too hot and crowded. That's okay. But if you describe someone's hometown or an actual restaurant as a slimy pit with no redeeming qualities, you'll risk offending readers who disagree.

If your story's location is a fictional place:

1. Have you created setting elements that make sense, even those for fantasy environments? ☐ yes ☐ no

2. Have you ensured created setting specifics don't work against other created features? ☐ yes ☐ no

 ACTION

Mentally go through the list of elements in the table above and recall what you've designed for each element. Record any that don't mesh with other elements.

Example:

In an arid environment, you have a murderer bury body parts in lush parks around town.

To give your setting a sense of authenticity, yet allow the elements your story requires, employ a combination of real and fictional settings:

- Use features of a real setting but give them fictional names.

- Create a fictional setting that is a composite of multiple real places.
- Design a fictional town within a real country or state.

If your story, usually a shorter work, focuses on the theme and the characters, it may require only limited description of the city, town, state, or country.

Example:

The entire story takes place in a building, a forest, or a neighborhood cul-de-sac.

Do you avoid blocks of description and show the elements of setting through your characters' interactions with the things that surround them? ☐ yes ☐ no

 ACTION

Locate up to three setting descriptions in your SAMPLE. Evaluate whether they are telling or showing. Then try viewing your characters' surroundings in each occurrence through an imaginary camera lens. Sweep your camera in a 360-degree view around your character. Write down what you saw. Choose the elements that will ground the reader as to where the characters are, show something about the characters, and work meaningfully with the plot. Now, through characters' actions and the POVC's thoughts, rewrite the descriptions that are telling.

Examples:

Setup:

Cleoman has had a frustrating conversation with her mother and has left the family hut to fume outside.

Telling:

The cloudless sky was azure. The ground in the village was hard, dry, and covered with a fine dust. A noisy blackbird perched on the top of the remainder of a charred tree irritated her. It was going to be a bad day.

Showing:

Cleoman blocked the sun with her hand and eyed the cawing blackbird perched atop what was left of a charred tree. She scooped up a stone from the ground as hard as Manman's washboard and hurled it toward the annoying bird. He lifted his shiny black head and cackled as the stone rose toward the azure sky, plummeted to earth, and sent up a cloud of fine dust at her feet.

 ACTION

Revisit those three setting occurrences edited in the last ACTION exercise. Add or replace descriptive phrases with words that evoke images and give the reader a sense of era, place, culture, or technology. Don't overdo; one word can speak volumes.

Be specific to evoke images:

- **Known landmarks:** Statue of Liberty; Eiffel Tower; Alamo
- **Communication devices:** smoke signals; black desk telephone; fax machine
- **Work-related items:** laser gun; plow and mule; Fortran data cards
- **Clothing:** gingham dress; polyester bikini; sari
- **Music:** minuet; country; reggae
- **Fad words:** swell; groovy; ballistic
- **Rooms:** lanai; parlor; media room
- **Buildings:** shack; palace; skyscraper
- **Events:** bubonic plague; gold rush; D-day
- **Jobs:** chimney sweep, backhoe operator, financial planner
- **Tools:** stone, hammer, nail gun

If a setting element is considered a character in your story, it will require intricate details.

Examples:

A haunted house, a hurricane, or a tradition passed down through generations could be considered a character in a story.

To avoid becoming repetitive, do you reduce descriptions to occasional references once the reader understands a setting? □ yes □ no

 ACTION

For the remainder of Day 6, review your no answers, and work on settings in your SAMPLE. Remember, you'll have time to work on the rest of the chapters during Days 20-30 with the help of a checklist.

RESOURCES

Writing the Breakout Novel: Insider Advice for Taking Your Fiction to the Next Level by Donald Maass

Season Your Story with Voice, Pace, and Humor

Your author's voice, a balanced pace, and touches of humor in the right places will make your scenes stand out.

This is the last chapter in which we'll focus on high-level aspects of your story. Although it takes writing, writing, writing to develop your voice, to get a good sense of pace, and to know when to use humor, today we'll look at some helps for each.

Writer's Voice

Writer's voice is the *you* that comes across in your story that makes your story unique. Your voice shows up when you relax and allow who you are to come through your writing. I'm not referring to author intrusion. We'll cover that topic later.

Most of us have social filters to protect us from saying something we know might offend someone or get us in trouble. Our filters take our real thoughts and clean them so our actions and words are what we think are acceptable to survive in our environment.

Alzheimer's disease erodes filters, and often people with the disease become blustery or mean. Or after spending years of being reserved or private, some become serene or friendly.

Because what goes on inside us is often different than what we say, do, or write, we writers need to create a second filter with bigger holes in the mesh. The second filter is one that allows us to be more honest with our readers. Our purpose is not to allow our inner snarky thoughts to develop unlikeable characters or to offend or hurt readers. Our purpose is to share who we are with our readers.

 ACTION

Choose a short scene in your SAMPLE and rewrite it like you were writing it for yourself alone. This doesn't mean the scene is necessarily better now, but look for the places in which you felt you were being more honest than usual and you liked what came out.

Did your POVC in the revised scene remain likeable? ☐ yes ☐ no

 ACTION

If no, use the ACTION under Unlikeable Protagonist in Chapter 2 to rewrite the character and her thoughts.

As you work on your SAMPLE in other ACTION exercises, let what you've learned about your voice come through.

Pace

You never want to receive reviews that say:

- Too much description and explaining bogged down the story. Often nothing was happening.
- Everything happened too fast, which left me wanting to know more about the characters.

Your story needs to continually move the plot forward. However, your story, especially thrillers, needs to give readers a rest after particularly intense scenes. A slower pace is one device to provide a short period for readers to collect their wits or reflect on what's happened.

Does your SAMPLE read at a comfortable pace, moving the plot along? ☐ yes ☐ no

 ACTION

Mark spots in your SAMPLE where the pace seems to bog down or is too rushed.

Tips to Increase Your Story's Pace

When needed, here are ways you can increase your stories pace, especially for chapters in Act 2:

- Insert an action scene with little description and no explanations. Perhaps you've been describing something or someone or explaining something to the reader. If the description or explanation is important, you can accomplish them through an action scene. Don't describe how Renee has courage to act, show Renee doing a courageous act.
- Spin the plot off into a new direction. If your story is crawling, brainstorm a situation that opens up a new set of problems and conflict. Don't drag out how Detective

Conner and his team do mundane tasks to find the killer; surprise the reader and have Conner learn his best friend on the team is being blackmailed for planting evidence.

- End a scene with a cliffhanger. All scenes should end with a hook to keep the reader turning pages. If something hasn't ruffled things up in a while, end a scene with a humdinger. When Millie asks her best friend for forgiveness for gossiping about her facelift, don't have her best friend hug and forgive her. Have her best friend say, "I'll forgive you, if you forgive me for spending yesterday with your boyfriend."

- Fire up the dialogue. Keep descriptions and speaker attributes to a minimum. Don't give inner thoughts of the POVC telling how he feels after each retort; let his words tell how he feels. Let the reader know who starts the conversation with a *said Barry* or a short beat, such as *Barry slapped the table*. Then make the dialogue rip from one character to another. In a longer dialogue, give another speaker attribute or brief beat in the middle to keep the reader grounded in who's speaking.

- Start scenes mid-action. You must ground the reader with who, when, what, and where at the beginning of a scene. Instead of telling that information, though, get into the action and feed information in through the characters' actions and dialogue.

- Summarize boring play-by-play paragraphs, situations unimportant to the story, and backstory. Don't tell the reader how Jerry moved from point A to point B; put him at point B with a few transition words. Don't spell out all the mundane things that happened during Jerry's week or year before the next important plot point arises; give a transition sentence and move him forward a week or a year. We've already talked about feeding in bits of backstory.

- Choose punchy action verbs with harsh consonant sounds. Don't write, He took the transmitter and descended the stairs; write, He grabbed the transmitter and clunked down the stairs. See how the second sentence picks up the pace?

- Write short chapters and scenes. This technique forces you to get to the purpose of each scene.

- Use short paragraphs or break up long paragraphs. Readers need to see space. Long paragraphs appear formidable and feel like drudgery to read.

 ACTION

Using the best solution from above, rewrite the sluggish spots you marked in your SAMPLE.

Humor

A slowed pace gives the reader a break after a tense scene, and humor can do the same. In detective TV shows, which deal with horrendous murders, humor is interjected after particularly gruesome scenes. Screenwriters understand viewers' needs to collect themselves, or they'll flip to another show.

Humor can also add spice and interest to a character or scene. But humor that is crass or forced can turn readers off.

Tips for Using Humor

- Sprinkle humor in and don't ever explain it.

- Humor should never take the reader out of the story.

- You can use humor in any situation as long as it feels like something that could happen in real life.

- Don't keep trying to make something funny that's

resisting you. It may be distasteful, need such extensive setup that it loses the reader, or too outdated to tickle modern readers.

- Don't create humor that's complicated and makes the reader work for his smile.
- Don't repeat witty humor, hoping that it'll work a second or third time. It most likely won't because it's lost the element of surprise.
- Don't include slapstick humor, i.e., clumsy actions or humorously embarrassing events, unless they're well planned, carefully orchestrated, and relate closely to the story.
- Don't use your story to tell all your favorite jokes. Readers are looking for story, not standup comedy. Sometimes you have to kill your darlings.
- Don't overdo the humorous moment in length or drama. Allow the humor to flow in naturally.

Devices to Create Humor

The examples for these humor devices come from my novel, *Calculated Risk*. They occur during Cisney and Nick's trip from Virginia to his family home in North Carolina. The two are colleagues. After Cisney's boyfriend dumps her, sympathetic Nick invites her to spend Thanksgiving with his family.

Exaggeration

Exaggerate a situation or a character's physical trait, behavior, or manner of speech.

Example:

Since when did a man's simple announcement of an ice cream choice thrill her to her toes? It was all in his delivery. And those eyes. And that dimple. Who'd have thought ice cream with an actuary required a surge protector?

Reversal

Set up a situation that creates a certain expectation from readers and then give a conclusion that violates their expectation. *Misdirection* is a shorter version of reversal when a sentence or paragraph is headed in an expected manner then changes direction and ends with a surprise. (He was tall, dark, and dumb.)

Example:

Okay," she said. "I've planned torture methods to get you to talk. I've counted eighteen mile markers, and I've tried to sleep, but now certain thoughts about a certain person are making me sad. I refuse to be gloomy."

He smiled. No, the woman wasn't boring. "You want to talk about it?" Had he really opened that door? Great. Let the Jason lamentations begin.

"Okay. Sometimes the mile markers seem as if they're more than a mile apart, and sometimes they seem spaced less than a mile. Do you think Virginia saves money by not hiring civil engineers? Do road workers just take a stab at when the next mile has been reached?"

You've read your SAMPLE in the Pace ACTION items above. Did humorous moments fit in naturally with the situations? ☐ yes ☐ no

 ACTION

If you answered *no*, remove or rewrite the humor. If you choose to rewrite humorous moments, use the above tips and devices so they don't seem dropped in, forced, or jarring.

You can address voice, pace, and humor in the pages beyond your SAMPLE in Days 20-30.

Congratulations! You have completed the first section of *Tailor Your Fiction Manuscript in 30 Days*. This completes the high-level examination of your story. In Section 2, we'll focus on building engaging scenes.

RESOURCES

The Fire in Fiction: Passion, Purpose, and Techniques to Make Your Novel Great by Donald Maass

Scenes: Book Building Blocks
Days 8 - 14

Make a Scene of Your Scene

Scenes are the main building blocks of your story.

In this chapter, you'll make sure your scenes have purpose and they're the right type of scenes. We'll cover how to improve scene plots, hooks, grounding the reader, flashbacks, transitions, and the ending hook. For some items, you'll work immediately on an ACTION. For others, you'll work on them at the end of this chapter. For both, you'll work on your SAMPLE only. I'll pose yes-or-no questions when necessary.

A Scene's Reasons to Exist

Require your scenes to have three purposes. If a scene has less than three, either cut it or rewrite it to give it three reasons to exist.

Essential Purposes

A scene should have at least one of the following essential purposes. The other purposes can be any reasons you wish.

- Progresses or changes the character's goals
- Adds conflict between characters
- Includes an event that strengthens or changes a character's motivation

Suppose you wrote a scene with the sole purpose of introducing a character. The heroine and the new character have a pleasant get-to-know-you conversation. The scene has no conflict or other purpose. Readers would likely skim this scene of pleasantries.

A good example of a scene with essential and nonessential purposes comes from the movie, *Leap Year*.

Example:

First, you'll need the setup. It's leap year. Jeremy is on business in Dublin. Anna follows him. She plans to propose to Jeremy on leap year day. When a problem forces Anna's airplane to land at an airport on the other side of Ireland from Dublin, she hires a reluctant local, Declan, to drive her to Dublin. During the trip, Declan claims that what's precious to a person is what he'd grab in the case of a fire. The two fall for each other by the time they reach Dublin, but Jeremy asks Anna to marry him as soon as they arrive. Anna makes what she thinks is the right choice and accepts.

Now in the example scene, Anna is back in the U.S. and engaged to Jeremy. They host a party in their classy apartment, which they've wanted since the beginning of the movie. During the party, Jeremy tells their friends that the old-fashioned owners of the building were concerned about their marriage status. He says, "Unmarried you're out; married you're in." So, he thought why not, and asked Anna to marry him. Anna's hurt and confused by his comment.

Anna engages the fire alarm. As guests leave the apartment, Anna watches Jeremy run to his office and collect his electronic devices. He never looks at Anna. She now knows where his heart lies.

Four reasons for this scene to exist are:

1. It shows Anna's goal to marry Jeremy has shifted to wanting him to marry her because he loves her. (essential purpose)

2. We see Jeremy's true motives for marriage. (essential purpose)

3. Jeremy's comment to their friends creates conflict. (essential purpose)

4. Her fire alarm experiment shows Anna where she stands with Jeremy and pushes the plot toward a new direction. Toward Declan.

Other Reasons for a Scene to Exist

- Moves the plot forward
- Reveals a secret
- Foreshadows an upcoming event
- Reveals an epiphany
- Turns the plot in a new direction
- Reveals a clue
- Increases the pace
- Raises stakes or makes them matter more
- Introduces a character
- Adds suspense
- Develops a character
- Supplies comic relief
- Bonds characters
- Introduces a new setting
- Shows a character's competency
- Wraps up a loose end
- Removes a character from the story
- Weaves in needed information

Types of Scenes

Stories should contain three types of scenes: action, reflection, and combination scenes. Employing these three types of scenes helps to insure your scene has three purposes, including at least one essential purpose.

Action Scenes

Action scenes have a goal, conflict, and a crisis moment. Obstacles get in the way of characters meeting their goals, which feeds the conflict and the crisis moment. Obstacles can be people, events, emotions, or secrets.

Example:

Suppose Tammy wants her friends to like her new boyfriend, Parker, who is different from her last boyfriend whom they disliked. (Goal)

Tammy drives. She collects her three friends, and after she picks up her third friend, Celia, she tells them she's invited Parker to join them for dinner and the movie. Her friends balk. They're unhappy that Parker will change how they normally have fun together. They claim she should have consulted them first. (Conflict/Obstacle)

They tell Tammy they can meet Parker sometime other than their girl's night out. They urge her to call Parker and tell him she'll go out with him another night. When she tells them she can't do that because Parker has looked forward to meeting them, they exit her car and pile into Celia's SUV. Tammy is hurt. She fears Parker will think she's a fool who has shallow friends. (Disaster)

Reflection Scenes

Reflection (or sequel) scenes have a response, dilemma, and decision. This may be a short scene.

Example:

While Tammy drives to the restaurant to meet Parker, she stews over her friends' uncooperativeness. Maybe they really are shallow. Then she looks at the situation from their viewpoint. Suppose Celia had done what she'd done. How would she feel? She realizes she was wrong to invite Parker to the girl's night out without asking her friends. (Response)

But she still has problems. What is she going to tell Parker? She wonders whether her friends have decided to dine at a different restaurant than planned to avoid her and Parker. If they show up at the planned restaurant, will they ignore her and Parker and sit at another table? She couldn't bear the humiliation. What would Parker think if she tells him the truth and asks him to go with her to another restaurant? He might want to end their date and go home. What should she do? (Dilemma)

She tells herself, trying to hide what she did to her friends is the same as starting a relationship with him in a lie. If Parker doesn't like the truth and leaves her, he's not the right man. She will tell him the truth and ask him to follow her to her favorite restaurant. (Decision)

Combination Scenes

Combination scenes begin with a short reflection passage and then transition to an action scene with a new goal, conflict, and crisis moment. Suppose Tammy's reflection scene is the opening for a combination scene. Let's pick up after her decision.

Tammy meets Parker at the originally planned restaurant. She tells him the truth, hoping he'll understand her mistake and they can enjoy their date at her favorite restaurant. (Goal)

Parker receives the truth graciously. He follows her to her favorite restaurant. However, it's also one of Celia's favorites, and Tammy sees her friends sitting at a table laughing and enjoying themselves. She performs an about-face and pushes Parker outside the restaurant. He wants to know what's going on. He's famished and would like to eat. Now. At this restaurant. (Conflict)

Celia, who saw Tammy at the hostess station, exits the restaurant, pulls Tammy aside, and says, "You always have to have your way. You couldn't just enjoy your new guy and let us have our fun. You had to follow us and make us spend the evening with your dull-looking boyfriend." (Disaster)

And the scene goes on.

 ACTION

For each scene in your SAMPLE, answer the following questions. Creating answer codes may be helpful in recording your responses, e.g. C1S1Q1 *no*, for Chapter 1, Scene 1, Question 1, Answer: no.

1. Does the scene contain at least one essential purpose concerning the character's goals, conflict, or motives? ☐ yes ☐ no

2. Does the scene have three purposes to exist? ☐ yes ☐ no

3. Is the first scene in Chapter 1 an action scene? ☐ yes ☐ no (For Chapter 1 only)

4. In an action scene, is the character's overall goal or the scene's goal clear? ☐ yes ☐ no

5. In an action scene, does meaningful conflict occur? ☐ yes ☐ no

6. In an action scene, does the conflict end up in a worse situation? ☐ yes ☐ no

7. Does some kind of reflection, response, or reaction follow an action scene in either a reflection scene or a combination scene? ☐ yes ☐ no

8. If the scene is a reflection scene, does it need to be a stand-alone scene? (No answer means it could be part of a combination scene.) ☐ yes ☐ no

9. In reflection moments, does a dilemma confront the character? ☐ yes ☐ no

10. In reflection moments, does the character make a decision, whether it's a good decision or not? ☐ yes ☐ no

ACTION

For each scene with one or more no answers, decide if the scene is necessary. If it's not, cut it. If it's necessary, rewrite it and address the problems the above questions revealed.

Cramming in Characters

A common first-chapter problem is introducing too many characters in the first scene. This can also be a problem for later scenes. A scene introducing several characters can make readers feel as if they've entered a gala with names thrown at them like confetti. Most readers can comfortably keep track of three characters at a time. With more, readers become confused and forget the characters' relationships to the protagonist.

Think of it like this: If you went to a party and met fifteen new people, would you expect to receive the full background of each person in that three-hour gathering? Probably not.

ACTION

Locate the scenes, if any, in your SAMPLE in which you introduced multiple characters in a scene:

- First, determine which characters are crucial to the story. If they don't have at least a short-term purpose, eliminate them.

- Also, consider combining two or more characters into one person.

- In the first chapter, allow only characters who support

the scene setup and who keep the focus on the protagonist.

- Decide which of the necessary characters can be introduced in a subsequent scene. This removes the first-scene overload and starts the story faster. The reader will have a chance to grasp the story setup first before bombarded with people. And this allows each character to have his personal cameo in a later scene.

- At the least, space introductions of essential characters throughout the scene and give each a memorable feature, action, or dialogue.

- Give characters names that sound different than other characters in the book.

Example:

Millie entered the living room, hoping she could survive Mom's wake. Millie's brother, Don, introduced his college roommate, Mark. Before Millie had a chance to say more than hello, Sally and Vera, her mother's closest friends, approached and threw their arms around Millie. Extricating herself from Mom's chums, Millie caught a glance of Ron over by the shrimp platter. She needed to speak to him. Of course, Mom's cousin, Emma, had to come. Emily, her daughter, followed her everywhere.

Let's evaluate the paragraph with some added information.

- Mark never enters the story again or has any purpose.

- Don and Ron and Emma and Emily are essential, but their names are too similar.

- Emma and Emily with their new names could be detained and arrive the following day.

- Although names and relationships are given, the reader has nothing memorable to associate with each character to keep the eight characters straight.

- Mom's chums could be combined into one friend.

Millie's chest caved. Couldn't Don have honored their mother and come to her wake sober? Millie turned her sisterly glare aimed at staggering Don into a smile as Mom's closest friend, Vera, approached with outstretched arms. Vera's arm flab flapped as she waddled closer. Extricating herself from Vera's bear hug, Millie caught sight of handsome Adam half hidden by the oriental screen. Was he avoiding their needed conversation?

Clichéd Scene Plots

We've tackled clichéd plots at the book level in Chapter 1. Let's address clichéd plots at the scene level. I'll list some overused actions or events. Most can be considered lazy writing.

Overused Scene Plots

1. The reader "sees" the character die, but he's really alive.

2. A time bomb with a digital readout has been set to go off in minutes.

3. A character's dream relays information or emotions.

4. The character looks in a mirror to describe herself.

5. A writer interrupts with, "little did he know," and ruins the suspense of future events.

6. Writer inserts an inside joke in connection with a TV show to impress his readers.

7. To quickly move the plot along, a character is knocked out and wakes elsewhere.

8. Cars are unlocked so characters can "borrow" them and escape with a full tank.

9. In fights atop trains, the hero is thrown off conveniently as the train crosses a river.

10. Given the opportunity, the villain doesn't kill the hero, because he may be useful later.

11. Characters told to stay back don't.

12. The hero chases and tickles heroine and then they gaze into each other's eyes.

13. The character wakes, shuts off the alarm, and gets ready for the day.

14. Car, boat, or foot chases.

 ACTION

If you've used actions or events similar to those in the table in your SAMPLE scenes, brainstorm some other possibilities or make the clichéd plots fresh. The extra work will be worth the results.

A man bringing his sick wife flowers is nice, but it's a cliché. See in the example below how a man bringing flowers can be made more touching and interesting.

Example:

Sarah struggled into a sitting position and rested her back against the headboard. If she didn't overcome this illness and help Clay in the field, they'd lose much of the crop. They still didn't know if the drought had damaged the wheat. Even with a good crop, the proceeds would barely pay their bills.

She slid her legs over the edge of the bed. When she stood, lightheadedness and nausea seized her, and her knees wobbled. Clay didn't need to come home and find her on the floor. He already spent too much time worrying about her slow progress. She crawled into bed.

As she stared out the window, a tear rolled to her jaw. In the distance, Clay strode in from the fields for lunch. She grabbed her comb from the bedside table and went to work on her tangled hair. Was that flowers he was carrying?

The front door opened and paper rustled in the other room. What was Clay doing?

Clay clumped into the bedroom and held out the flowers concealed in a sheet of her art paper. His lips trembled, and he looked as if he was about to cry. What had Clay done wrong that brought on rare tears and flowers?

Studying his face for a clue, she accepted his guilt offering. Her fingers shook as she unwrapped a posy of … healthy green wheat.

First-Chapter Hook

Your opening lines may determine whether an editor reads further or a reader buys your book.

A first-chapter opening *is not*

- telling what the character's life has been like up to this point,
- describing the town where the character lives,
- relating his morning routine,
- giving the details of the rooms in his house,
- describing his breakfast, or
- detailing the lovely view from his window.

Why should I care about what you have to say? Sounds rude, doesn't it. But that's what readers want to know when they approach your book. Your opening lines needs to hook your reader, making him want to learn what's going to happen in your story.

Your opening line should contain a hint of mystery and originality. It should raise a question for readers.

Does the opening line of your book have a hint of mystery and does it provoke a question? ☐ yes ☐ no

 ACTION

Whether you answered yes or no, review the opening line of your book. Write the question the reader will have concerning your story. If it's not a reader-engaging question, rethink and rewrite the line until the reader would ask a probing question.

> **Examples:**
> First lines with no mystery:
> 1.   The sun was out full force.
> 2.   I live in California.
> 3.   My name is Dawn.

In the last example, a reader most likely wouldn't ask, "Why is her name Dawn?" The reader's question must be one of genuine curiosity.

Let's improve on these first lines.

> 1.   For the first time in a year, Hector saw the sun, and it was out in full force. (Why hadn't Hector seen the sun in a year?)
> 2.   Due to an accident, I live in California. (What accident caused the protagonist to live in California?)
> 3.   Because of what happened at the first glimmer of light on the day I was born, my name is Dawn. (What happened at the first glimmer of light? Did the event have something to do with Dawn, her mother, or the town?)

This next example is from my short story, "Plotting Murder."

> With the many interruptions to Margo Kawalski's already loaded schedule, when would she find the time to kill Rita? (How can Margo act so casual about murder? And why would she want to kill Rita?)

Grounding the Reader

In every scene, you must let the reader know

- who's in the scene as the scene opens;
- whose POV the scene is in;
- where these characters are;
- when it occurs compared to the ending of the prior scene; and
- what's the mood of the scene.

If you don't supply this information in the first few sentences, the reader will feel like she's awakened from a coma. However, don't describe or explain the Who, Where, When, and Mood. Always start the scene mid-action and show these grounding elements through characters' actions, thoughts, senses, or dialogue. For example, reveal the Where (scene setting) through what the POVC reacts to, sees, hears, and does.

 ACTION

Review the first few paragraphs of each scene in your SAMPLE. Through actions, thoughts, senses, and dialogue, add the grounding elements (Who, Whose POV, Where, When, and Mood) you've left out.

The following example is the first paragraph from my romance, *Calculated Risk*, Chapter 6, Scene 1. The reader already knows from earlier scenes that Nick invited colleague Cisney to his family's home for the weekend out of sympathy, because she'd been dumped by her boyfriend and had nowhere to go for Thanksgiving.

Example:

Nick raised his bowed head. The peacefulness of Dad's blessing turned into a hubbub of chatter and clinking silverware as the family passed serving dishes around the table. Nick held a bowl for Cisney. While she concentrated on transferring sweet potatoes to her plate, he studied her face. Her transformation from the frazzled woman down by the lake into the composed beauty sitting next to him was amazing. The light scent of her exotic perfume mixed with turkey aroma.

The scene before this one ends with Cisney and Nick's cousin, Tony, leaving the dining room after they've had a playful, get-to-know-each-other interaction while setting the table for Thanksgiving dinner.

Note the scene begins mid-action and the reader knows from this first opening paragraph.

- The scene is from Nick's POV. (Who)
- The family is at the dining room table for a meal. (Who, Where)
- The mood is festive with the hubbub of chatter. (Mood)
- Cisney is sitting next to Nick. (Who, Where)
- The food indicates that it's the expected Thanksgiving meal. (What, When)
- Cisney has changed significantly from a prior scene. (Mood, Hook)
- He notices her light perfume scent. (Mood, Hook)

Notice I didn't tell the Who, Where, When, and Mood. They happened through what Nick observed and the family's actions (praying, chattering, and passing dishes).

Also, a hook is imbedded. Nick, a very private, analytical, closed-mouth person, who's not interested in a relationship with any woman, notices Cisney is a "beauty" and smells nice. The reader will want to know if he might be changing his mind about his colleague.

Flashbacks

Don't use flashback unless you must. If your story alternates between past and present periods, you'll use flashbacks of sorts. Sometimes, you can't provide crucial information any other way. And, flashbacks can be a more dramatic way to provide backstory than a present character telling what happened. Also, a flashback may work for a prologue, to reveal something essential to the current story that happened earlier in the protagonist's life or in the story world.

Reasons to Avoid Flashbacks

- They're info dumps of old news stemming from an author's wish to explain everything.
- They're a cop-out to avoid writing difficult present story.
- They tell information that can be fed into current scenes a little at a time through dialogue and the POVC's internal thoughts.
- Long flashbacks may indicate that the main story should have started earlier.
- Flashbacks usually halt the current story, distract the reader, and cause her to lose interest. Readers are interested in the forward progress of the current story.
- Flashbacks remove suspense of why something happened in the past, ending the reader's desire to know the secret.
- They exist for no good reason. A flashback that is merely an interesting story from a character's biography is not a good reason.

General Tips for Writing Necessary Flashbacks

- Don't include more than one or two flashbacks.
- Use flashbacks only after the reader is engaged in the

story and knows the character (after several scenes).

- Reserve flashbacks until the reader must know the information—keep the suspense going.
- Make sure the flashback moves the main story forward.
- Give long flashbacks their own chapter or scene.
- Include goals, motivations, and resolutions like in any other scene.
- Place flashbacks after exciting scenes so the reader will want to return to the main story.

Specific Tips for Writing Necessary Flashbacks

- Give the character a trigger that takes him into the flashback—he sees an object, smells a scent, or experiences an action.
- Use the past perfect tense (had lived) as the character enters the flashback for stories written in the past tense. After the first sentence or two, switch to past tense until near the end of the flashback. Before exiting the flashback, change to past perfect a few times. After leaving the flashback, return to past tense. (Limits the cumbersome past perfect tense.)
- Use the simple past during the entire flashback for stories written in the present tense.
- Limit the flashback to key moments.
- Show what shaped the characters into who they are now or show what the past story world was like. After the flashback and as the present story moves forward, the reader should see the character or story world from a new perspective.
- Write ending sentences that transition the reader and character back to the present. For example, use a trigger that calls them into the present (a doorbell). The trigger can be abrupt or one that eases them back into the present.

ACTION

Locate any flashbacks in your SAMPLE. Using the reasons against flashbacks above, determine whether the flashbacks are necessary. If they are important, use the tips to make them work better in your story.

Suspension of Belief

Disbelief wrenches the reader from the story. The problem may be that the character's excessive or dramatic emotions (or lack of emotions) don't match the seriousness of events. Or the character has knowledge or a super power that was never set up or hinted at previously.

Examples of actions that cause readers' suspension of belief:

1. A senior citizen, who has had triple-bypass surgery two weeks earlier, helps carry an injured person.

2. Hero and heroine come to a wide river they must cross. He says, "Don't worry, I was an Olympic swimmer."

3. A loving mother flirts with an old flame at her son's funeral.

4. A man has sprained fingers and opens a honey jar.

5. A widow who loved her husband dearly is ready to start dating after three months.

6. Hero suddenly knows how to dismantle a car engine and put it back together.

7. A woman who has never ridden on a motorcycle mounts a Harley and chases a car.

8. A nonmedical woman sews up a fugitive's wound without flinching.

9. Heroine needs blackmail money, and a generous check arrives in the mailbox.

10. A woman tearfully mourns inside her house for days after losing her pet turtle.

 ACTION

Locate any unbelievable actions, dialogue, and events in your SAMPLE and either remove them or set them up earlier in the story.

Here's a rewrite of an example from the above table: *A nonmedical woman sews up a fugitive's wound without flinching.*

Example:

Clara handed the man, who'd said his name was Jake, the only spool of thread she had.

His two-inch wound gaped, jagged and bloody. She winced.

Jake negotiated the green thread through the needle's eye. "Okay, Clara, I need you to sew the gash together. Put in about eight stitches an eighth of an inch from each edge."

Clara stepped back, shaking her head. "I can't."

"You've got to, Clara. I'll hold the sides together." He extended the needle toward her. "You can do this, Clara. Pretend you're sewing a tear in one of your blouses."

Clara took the needle, her hand shaking. Okay. This was going to be as simple as mending the blue blouse in the rag pile in her closet.

She sat on the chair across from Jake, swallowed, lowered the needle, and pushed its point into his flesh. Her eyes closed as she retched.

And the scene goes on.

Actions Trump Thoughts and Feelings in Showing the Hero's Character

Actions mean decisions have been made. Decisions that have been made reveal character. The first example below gives only thoughts. The second example provides only actions and shows how the reader can understand Sylvia better than when only her thoughts are given. The third example combines actions and thoughts and displays a well-rounded picture of Sylvia.

Example:

Solely Sylvia's thoughts:

Six months without Brent? No job was worth that sacrifice. How could Brent even consider taking the position Mr. Halbreth offered? Brent was being selfish. What if he had a heart attack in the jungle? He'd die before anyone could transport him to civilization? Right now, she could strangle Brent—and Mr. Halbreth.

Solely Sylvia's actions:

Mr. Halbreth stood as Sylvia entered his office. He gestured toward a chair. "Please, have a seat, Mrs. Russell."

She sat and crossed her legs. "I hope I'm doing the right thing, Mr. Halbreth."

"What's on your mind?"

"What I'm about to tell you, Mr. Halbreth, my husband would never reveal to you, because he wants the job."

"We want him."

Sylvia ran her tongue over her lips. "Brent has a heart condition."

Mr. Halbreth's confident smile flattened.

Sylvia hurried on. "If he has a heart attack, he needs to be near a hospital equipped to save his life."

"On his application, Brent indicated he had only borderline high blood pressure."

"Of course he would." She stood. "I must go." She planted her forefinger on his desk and captured his gaze. "Hopefully, you have an alternate candidate."

Sylvia's retreating, high-heeled footsteps echoed in the silence.

No matter what her thoughts or feelings are, Sylvia has gone behind Brent's back to sabotage the offer. This says much about how far she'll go to get her way. Let's add Sylvia's thoughts to the scene to show whether she's cold-bloodedly or desperately betraying Brent.

Combination of Sylvia's actions and thoughts:

Mr. Halbreth stood as Sylvia entered his office. He gestured toward a chair. "Please, have a seat, Mrs. Russell."

She sat and crossed her legs. "I hope I'm doing the right thing, Mr. Halbreth." Could he hear her heart thudding as she carried out the hardest job in her life?

"What's on your mind?"

"What I'm about to tell you, Mr. Halbreth, Brent would never reveal to you, because he wants the job."

"We want him."

So did she. She ran her tongue over her lips. *This is for us, Brent.* She drew in a breath. "My husband has a heart condition."

Mr. Halbreth's confident smile flattened.

Good. She had his attention.

Sylvia hurried on. "If he has a heart attack, he needs to be near a hospital equipped to save his life."

"On his application, Brent indicated he had only borderline high blood pressure."

"Of course he would." She stood. "I must go." She planted her forefinger on his desk and captured his gaze. "Hopefully, you have an alternate candidate." Had he understood what she wanted him to do?

Sylvia's retreating, high-heeled footsteps echoed in the silence. Heaven forgive her. But she'd done what was necessary. Now, she'd hustle home and prepare Brent's favorite lasagna for dinner.

POV Shifts (Head Hopping)

Confusion arises when the author gets inside multiple characters' heads during a scene. Head hopping can throw the reader out of the story while he shifts to the viewpoint of a different character. This transferring to other viewpoints distances the reader from the characters and prevents him from building rapport with any character.

Stick to one POV in each scene. If you must shift to another character's POV within a scene, switch only once, follow the suggestions in the next section titled Transitions, and remain in the second character's POV until the end of the scene.

Example:

Nancy approached Sarah. When Sarah saw her, would she veer off in another direction? (Nancy's POV)

Sarah lifted her hand in a weak wave. That was promising. (Nancy's POV)

Sarah decided to give Nancy one more chance. Nancy didn't deserve it, but they'd been best friends once. (Sarah's POV)

They stopped within arm's reach of each other. What was her next step?

See how we're confused as to which woman is questioning her next step?

Often the thoughts of one of the characters are unnecessary. You can show that character's feelings through her:

- Dialogue
- Facial expressions
- Actions

Example:

Nancy approached Sarah. When Sarah saw her, would she veer off in another direction?

Sarah lifted her hand in a weak wave. That was promising.

They stopped within arm's reach of each other. What should she do? Hug Sarah? Apologize?

Sarah's gaze flitted away then returned. "You hurt me, Nancy. But we've been best friends for too long not to give you another chance."

Nancy swallowed. The chunk of pride stuck in her throat before it went down.

"I don't deserve another chance."

Sarah's bottom lip trembled. "No, you don't, but I'd miss your good qualities. So, I forgive you."

 ACTION

Search your SAMPLE for places where you could show your POVC's decisions through her actions as well as through her thoughts. The action required may need only a sentence or two. At the same time, look for head hopping within scenes. For head hopping instances, decide whether a non-POVC's thoughts are necessary. If they're trivial, eliminate them. Otherwise, for the non-POVC, rewrite necessary thoughts into dialogue and show feelings through his facial expressions, gestures, and actions. If it's necessary to switch to another character's POV, follow the suggestions in the next section.

Transitions

Within a scene, readers need smooth transitions in moving to a new time or switching to another character's POV. Add an extra line to alert the reader that the time or POVC is changing. Then give the reader the information she needs to mentally switch gears. Make sure the reader knows:

- Who the POVC is now.
- What time of day or night it is now.
- Where the character is.

When moving to a new time or changing to a new POVC, make sure the time is later, even if only by a few seconds. If it's not, the reader will feel the story is going backward.

ACTION

If you have necessary time or POVC changes within your SAMPLE scenes, make sure you've added an extra line before the change and transitioned the reader to the new situation.

The following example shows a switch from Ann's POV to Jerry's in a scene. The setting remains the same, and the switch is immediately after Ann's last thought.

Example:

Poor transition:

Ann sighed. Hopefully, Jerry understood why she had to continue to wait for Henry's return.

Would Ann ever accept that Henry wasn't coming back? She'd said he'd been gone six years. What made her think he'd leave whatever life he'd set up for himself and come back to her after such a long time?

Better transition:

Ann joined Jerry in the den. Was he as upset as he looked?

Jerry lifted the framed photo from the mantel and studied Henry's image.

She walked to his side. Hopefully, he understood why she had to continue to wait for Henry's return. She reached for the photo.

(note the blank line here for POV switch)

Jerry gave the photo to Ann. Would Ann ever accept that Henry wasn't coming back? She'd said he'd been gone six years. What made her think Henry would leave his new life and come back to her after such a long time?

The rest of the scene remains in Jerry's POV.

End-of-Scene Hook

BLaH BUSTER

Prevent the reader from inserting a bookmark at the end of the scene and turning off the light. Instead, hook 'em. Whether the character's situation is bad or good, don't end the scene with quiet closure. End the scene with a cliffhanger or a reason for the reader to keep reading. Be careful, though. The hook must not be a gimmick but something integral to the story.

Also, the hook's "mystery" should be addressed the next time one or more of the characters in the current scene show up in a later scene. Don't leave characters hanging indefinitely.

 ACTION

Review the scene endings in your SAMPLE. Rethink those that don't lure the reader to the next scene. Make sure your ending hooks are an integral part of the story.

Examples:

Yawn producers:

- Tomorrow was another day.
- She smiled. "You've made me happy today, Mark."
- Kala leaned against the wall of her hiding place and went to sleep.

Below are the yawn producers rewritten into cliffhangers. Note how the writer can also brainstorm ways to prolong the reader's suspense about the cliffhangers.

Cliffhangers or the like:

- Tomorrow she'd tell him the reason she was guilty.
  (In the next scene in which these two are together again, she reveals the reason she was guilty. Or, the writer postpones telling the reason she's guilty in a satisfactory way, e.g., tomorrow the hero gets shipped out, and they don't meet.)
- (In Mark's POV.) She smiled. "You've made me happy today, Mark." Her smile faded. "I'm afraid that's a problem." Her cell rang. She lifted it to her ear, waved to him, and strode to her car. (In the next scene, Mark reflects on what she said, he's fearful that she's not free to have

a relationship with him and decides to call her tomorrow for the truth. Then in the call, she promises she'll tell him in person after class the next day.)

- Kala sat on the cold cement and leaned against the wall of her hiding place. Would someone have a reason to come down to the basement before morning? Was it safe to sleep? A ticking sounded. Mice? Or … (In the next scene Kala appears, she wakes from troubled sleep to footsteps descending the basement stairs.)

RESOURCES

GMC: Goal, Motivation & Conflict: The Building Blocks of Good Fiction by Debra Dixon

Hooked: Write Fiction That Grabs Readers at Page One and Never Lets Them Go by Les Edgerton

Add Suspense to Your Scenes – Scary or Otherwise

Wherever possible, add an element of suspense to your scenes to tantalize the reader.

Suspense in your story can be something other than sinister. It can be something the reader wants to know and looks forward to discovering.

Suspense Techniques for Any Genre

Here are five ways you can add suspense to a scene in any genre. ("21 Fast Hacks to Fuel Your Story with Suspense" by Elizabeth Sims, Writer's Digest, November/December 2014) To keep the examples short, I'll tell them in synopses.

1. Led to the Unknown

Character 1 leads Character 2 to a place unrevealed to the reader and Character 2. Character 2 experiences angst or anticipation, upping the reader's desire to know where they're going and what will be there. At the unknown place, a worthy payoff must exist, one that causes conflict, disaster, or Character 2 being deeply touched.

Example:

Daniel returns from visiting his sick father, who has recovered sooner than expected.

Belinda is surprised to see Daniel. She acts nervous and reluctant to let Daniel inside, but she steps aside, and he enters. He smells cigarette smoke and wonders if she has male company.

Daniel is disappointed at her reception. She hides her hands behind her back. He fears she didn't like the emerald ring he gave her and has taken it off.

When he asks if something's going on, she looks ashamed. Now he fears she's changed her mind about their relationship while he was away.

Belinda takes his hand and leads him upstairs. He's never been beyond the first floor and wonders what her intentions are.

To keep up the suspense for the reader, have an obstacle keep them from getting where they're going too quickly.

As they climb the stairs, the cigarette odor becomes stronger. Daniel stops and tells her she doesn't have to show him what's going on, just tell him. Looking distressed, she says she can't and leads him farther up the stairs.

He can't believe she'd be so cruel as to introduce her new boyfriend in her bedroom. As they continue up the stairs, he sweats.

At the top of the stairs, she veers from her bedroom and leads him into her bathroom. A plumber lies on the tile floor under dismantled sink pipes with a cigarette hanging from his lips. The plumber says, "Sorry, miss, no luck."

Belinda sadly shows Daniel her bare ring finger. His body caves, and he blows out a breath, clearly relieved. She looks confused. Suddenly, her eyes grow wide then flash. She accuses him of thinking she'd been entertaining a man in her bedroom. Belinda is furious.

If Belinda had shown him her new bedspread had a hole in it, the readers would feel cheated. If Belinda hadn't been angry that Daniel thought so little of her virtues, the payoff would be much less.

2. Future Plan Revealed

Character 1 tells Character 2 his plan for a future event. The future event causes Character 2 anxiety. The reader can share in the character's stress while eager to know what will happen. The future event can be something good, and then the reader looks forward to progressing to the event.

Example:

Two weeks before their wedding, Reese leaves Lacey a voicemail, that he must call off the wedding. He provides no explanation, and he goes off the grid.

The next day, Reese texts Lacey that he'll meet her at their bench in the park at 3:00 PM to reveal why he called off the wedding.

To build suspense, insert a scene or an incident that will delay the reader from finding out the reason Reese called off the wedding.

Right after Lacey receives the text, Lacey's best friend, Mandy, arrives. Lacey shares Reese's text and her hopes that the relationship can be mended. Reluctantly, Mandy confides that she saw Reese yesterday. He was with a blonde at the mall food court and was in such an intense discussion he didn't see Mandy.

Now, Lacey fears all is lost and wonders how long he's been two-timing his forever fiancée—her.

At 3:00, Lacey approaches their bench in the park. The blonde is with Reese. Lacey doesn't know whether to go boldly forward or run. Reese sees her and jogs across the grass to her on the path.

Reese tells Lacey his marriage to the blonde, Eva, was never annulled as they thought it had been when they were sixteen. Reese is still married to Eva. And now, Eva wants to stay married to Reese.

If Eva had been willing to pursue the easy solution of legally ending the marriage, the payoff to the reader would be less. With her desire to stay married, she causes new conflict.

3. Repeat Disaster Setup

For this suspense method, set up a potential disaster. The reader worries the disaster will happen, but it doesn't. Set up the same possible disaster again. The reader and the character fret that the disaster will occur. It doesn't. Set up the same disaster a third time. The reader has become leery that the disaster will ever happen. The reader relaxes. Then it happens much worse than feared for a significant reader payoff.

Example:

At the end of her best friend's wedding weekend, Jessica sits in the airport waiting area for her departing flight. She's relieved the weekend is over because she made a fool of herself. She pretended she was still a marketing rep for a big company, something glitzier than her current preschool-teacher profession, to entice handsome groomsman, Matthew. In record time, he ferreted out the truth. Mortified, she spent the last evening of the festivities in her hotel room, lonely, embarrassed, and crying.

Now, Jessica spots Matthew among the airport crowd walking past her seating section. If he sees her, she knows he'll come over and belittle her in his arrogant, offhanded way. She buries her nose in her book, her heart knocking against her ribcage. She peeks over the top of the book and sees him enter an airport restaurant.

Several minutes later, Jessica looks up from peacefully reading her book and sees Matthew in the crowd going in the opposite direction. He veers toward her seating section. She bends over and unzips her backpack, pretending to search for something inside. Hyperventilating, she prays the airline reps call the passengers of her flight to board now. Out of the corner of her eye, she watches Matthew's approaching feet. Matthew stops, throws his soda cup in a trashcan, and then reenters the crowd.

When the flight rep calls her zone to board, Jessica looks behind her. Matthew is coming toward her section. She scoots to the boarding line and stands in front of a large man. On the airplane, her heart rate returns to normal. She's safe. She sits in the window seat next to an older gentleman and shoves her backpack under the seat in front of her. When she straightens, Matthew stands next to the man, his gaze bearing down on her. "Would you mind trading seats with me, sir? I know this woman."

4. Set Up a Disaster Earlier

In an earlier scene, set up a situation that could be a potential disaster later. Make sure the setup is memorable and the consequences are important so the reader will worry the disaster will happen. And, of course, it does.

Example:

The heroine's husband, Doug, doesn't want children. He's out of town in this scene. Jenna takes a home pregnancy test, and it's positive. Upset and excited, she needs time to prepare her husband for the news—and brace herself for the nasty fallout. She throws the positive pregnancy test device into the trashcan because garbage day is tomorrow, and her husband won't return until the day after.

The device—the evidence of her pregnancy—inside the trashcan is the setup for a possible disaster. Now, we need to make the reader wait and fret.

Jenna's nosey, gossipy sister visits. Jenna prays her sister won't wander into the en suite bathroom as she sometimes does.

Hopefully, the reader will worry along with Jenna about her sister finding the pregnancy test device.

Jenna's sister leaves, without discovering the device. In the next scene on the same day, Doug comes home two days early. Dog-tired, he goes immediately into the bathroom. Jenna follows him and eyes the device in the trashcan. While Doug gets ready for bed, she stands in front of the trashcan and keeps him talking about his day. As soon as he's asleep, she plans to get rid of the device.

Doug completes his nighttime routine and ushers her out of the bathroom. She breathes easier. Doug turns back to throw a tissue into the trashcan, and says, "What's this?"

5. Facing Fear Alone

Arrange for the protagonist to face a potentially unpleasant situation alone.

Example:

Renee house-sits at her aunt's cottage. Woods surround the house. A long dirt road is the only access to the house. Renee jumped at the chance to be alone for the weekend because she needs to decide if she can trust Danny with her heart.

With a mug of cinnamon tea in her hand, she settles on the couch to pray about her relationship. A light beam streaks through the front window. Renee startles and spills hot tea on her jeans. Her heart beating wildly, she sets the mug on the coaster, and creeps to the window. Has her aunt returned early? Mustering her courage, she peeks out. The dim light from the small porch lamp reveals, Danny's stalking ex-girlfriend emerging from an SUV.

 ACTION

Using one of the five methods presented above, create at least one suspenseful situation within your SAMPLE or improve suspenseful moments that already exist.

Melodrama

Scenes should be dramatic. Readers want to live through events with characters and experience characters' emotions. Melodrama takes characters' emotions over the top and stresses plot or actions at the expense of characterization.

When characters' reactions are too exaggerated, they can separate the character from real-life emotions and take the reader out of the story. Melodrama can show up in situations other than suspenseful events, such as humorous moments or arguments.

Avoid using adverbs, screaming, and exclamation points. Doing the work to lead the reader through the character's reasonable emotions will wow the reader.

Tips to Tone Down Melodrama:

- Avoid clichéd reactions.

- When showing a character's emotions think understated, flattened, and subtle.

- Get inside your character and find behavior signs she'd display, even if she tries to hide her feelings.

- Listen to your character telling you she wouldn't react like that.

- Make a list of reactions from extreme to mild. Choose the reaction that is most appropriate for the character's personality and one that's believable.

- Don't allow intense, or even reasonable, reactions to drag on, even if they would in real life.

Example:

Timid Alice has had her last chance to show she's capable of handling her dream job. Her boss fires her. Here are possible reactions, listed from extreme to mild. She:

1. kneels, sobbing and begging for another chance;

2. wails that the boss is unreasonable and unfair;

3. marches from the office in a huff;

4. turns lifeless eyes to her boss, rises, walks to the door, rests her hand on the doorknob for a moment, straightens her back, and leaves; or

5. remains seated in the chair with her head bowed and one tear escaping her eye.

These are only a few possibilities. Whether she's fearful, angry, or stunned, the first two will distract the reader from what is going on inside normally timid Alice. Reaction 3 is less melodramatic but could be expanded to better show Alice's emotions. The last reaction shows her sadness and a hint of shame, but it shows no progression of her feelings. Reaction 4 shows how she runs through her feelings in a subtle manner:

All is lost → no need to stay → maybe she should express an opinion → decides not to → leaves with her dignity intact.

 ACTION

For any instances of melodrama in your SAMPLE, use the tips given above and tone down characters' over-the-top reactions.

Examples:

A woman discovers her husband stabbed to death in bed. See how the second example is more dramatic, but less melodramatic.

Melodramatic:

Mildred ran through the neighborhood, waving her arms and screaming.

Dramatic:

Mildred huddled in the corner of the bedroom, her breaths coming in shallow pants, her eyes focused on Harry's hand hanging off the side of the bed. The phone receiver lies on the floor beside her, emitting muted words from the 911 operator.

The second example brings the reader into the character's body reactions and decisions. Mildred has done her duty in calling 911, but she's now so stunned at what's happened that she stares at Harry's hand and doesn't hear the operator trying to communicate with her.

Or, the scene could have Mildred on the phone with the 911 operator, trying her best to answer the operator's questions while holding herself together. What's important is that Mildred's reactions must tie to Mildred's personality and make sense to the reader.

RESOURCES

Writing the Breakout Novel: Insider Advice for Taking Your Fiction to the Next Level by Donald Maass

★ CHAPTER ★
Seven

Lure Readers to Commit Identity Theft with Your Characters

Diving deeper into a character's point of view draws the reader into the character's mind, body, feelings, and senses.

In this chapter, you'll work on creating a closer connection between the reader and your POVC.

Intimacy Between Readers and Point-of-View Characters

Whether you write in first, second, or third person, you can increase intimacy between your reader and character by using the following six tips associated with writing in *deep point of view* (DPOV).

DPOV is concerned with a character's thoughts, not his dialogue. As you write your POVC's thoughts, you, as the author, step out of the scene and allow your POVC to think his thoughts. For your reader's sake, your job is to present only the important thoughts that advance the story. No run-on internal dialogue. And only rare italicized direct thoughts. Here are the tips.

1. Remain in the Now

Your character doesn't know the future. Keep your character's thoughts in the present and his actions linear. In DPOV, your character only knows his own thoughts, his current stimulus, and then his reaction. So, unfold events as they occur. No phrase, such as *Before the fateful telephone call* ... appears in DPOV. That would be a case of author intrusion.

Take the reader through what happens step by step. You won't show every movement; that would be boring. Your character can think about the past and the future, but only in the context of what's happening now.

Example:

Not linear:

Brody took pleasure in his meal. He planted a heaping spoonful of corn on his plate, after Ann passed him the creamed corn. Ann stared at him, smiling, when he glanced up from shoveling in corn.

Deep and linear:

Ann passed Sam the creamed corn. He planted a heaping spoonful on his plate. What a feast. He sampled the mashed potatoes. Mmm. Nothing could be creamier. Sinking his teeth into a fried chicken breast, he closed his eyes. To die for. If only Mom could cook like this. He glanced up from shoveling in corn. Ann stared at him, smiling.

In the deep and linear version, we aren't told Brody took pleasure in his meal; we enjoy it along with him through his thoughts and actions, which happen as he experiences them.

For more examples, see **Nonlinear Actions** in Chapter 10.

2. Don't Intrude

Don't tell the reader that a POVC

- thought,
- wondered,
- realized,
- decided,
- wished,
- hoped, or
- knew.

In DPOV, the author doesn't state these or use them as "thinker" attributes. She allows her POVCs to simply think, wonder, realize, decide, wish, hope, or know.

Example:

Telling:

Craig looked away. He thought Lee Ann was being unreasonable. He grabbed his keys and headed for the door.

Or

Craig looked away. Lee Ann was being unreasonable, he thought. He grabbed his keys and headed for the door. (here *thought* is used as a "thinker" attribute)

Test it:

In your head, you probably wouldn't think:

Lee Ann is being unreasonable, I think. ("thinker" attribute)

Or

I think Lee Ann is being unreasonable.

Intimate:

Craig looked away. Lee Ann was being unreasonable. He grabbed his keys and headed for the door.

Allow your characters to think without you intruding to tell the reader they're thinking. It's okay to use words from the list above in dialogue. *"I think John's depressed. What do you think?"*

More Examples:

Telling:

He *thought* Mary was mean. He *wished* she'd leave town, but he *realized* she wouldn't. So, he *decided* he would avoid the battle-ax.

Test it:

In your head, you probably wouldn't think:

I think Mary is mean. I wish she'd leave town, but I realize she won't. I decide I will avoid the battle-ax.

Intimate:

Mary was mean. If only she'd leave town, but no way would that happen. From now on, he'd avoid the battle-ax. (In this case, you might think, *I wish she'd leave town*, so you could use *wish* instead of *if only*.)

Telling:

She thought his idea stunk.

Intimate:

His idea stunk.

Telling:

She wondered why her father wouldn't let her attend the party.

Intimate:

Why wouldn't Daddy let her go to the party?

Turn the *wonder* cases into a question. Also, she wouldn't think *my father*; she'd think Daddy or whatever she calls her father.

Telling:

She wished she could start the day over.

Intimate:

If only she could start the day over.

For *wished*, *wanted*, and *hoped*, try *if only* now and then.

Telling:

She knew she couldn't make a living as a waitress.

Intimate:

She couldn't make a living as a waitress.

Or

Waitressing couldn't support her. There had to be something else she could do.

Or

No way could she make a living as a waitress.

For phrases, such as *she knew* (or *realized*) *she couldn't*, occasionally try *no way could she*. Sometimes we think, *I knew I was right*. So *knew* and *wished* work in DPOV.

Telling:

Snow covered the yard, so Cody decided to stay home.

Intimate:

Snow covered the yard. Halleluiah! A perfect day to stay home and read.

Telling:

Sara realized she had no place to go and feared she'd end up homeless.

Intimate:

She had no place to go. Sara wrung the strap of her empty handbag, her stomach cramping. If she ended up homeless, how would she survive?

3. Don't Tell an Emotion

Show the POVC's emotions using her body reactions, her actions, her thoughts, and her dialogue. (Also see Show, Don't Tell in Chapter 10.)

Don't name a feeling, such as anger, calmness, peace, or sadness. Instead, give thoughts, actions, and behaviors that accompany the feeling.

Examples:

Telling:

Angry, Ella slammed the door.

Intimate:

Heat rose up her neck. She balled her fists and glared at her accuser. What right did he have to speak to her like that? None. Absolutely none. She strode from the room and slammed the door.

Telling:

Struggling to breathe as he died, Mitchell felt an amazing calmness.

Intimate:

Mitchell's breaths came in shallow spurts. So, this was the end. He'd be gone in minutes. Not so scary. Freeing. He'd be with Jesus before the first star twinkled.

Telling:

Peace seeped through her. Everything would be okay.

Intimate:

Her heartbeats slowed to a steady rhythm. Where had the bags of potatoes on her shoulders gone? Hopefully, they'd been whipped into mashed potatoes. She chuckled. Yes. Everything would be okay.

Telling:

Sadness took over and hurt my work.

Intimate:

How long had I been staring at the pie charts? They might as well have been in Chinese. My tears made them blurry anyway. When would I ever be able to focus on anything again?

4. Don't State that the Point-of-View Character Is Using Her Senses

This is also called *filtering*. As above for "thinker" attributes, allow your character to simply see, hear, touch, taste, and smell.

Examples:

Telling:

I heard the stairs creak. I turned toward the staircase.

Intimate:

The stairs creaked. I turned toward the staircase.

Telling:

He saw the hounds racing toward the intruders. He wondered if he should call the dogs off.

Intimate:

The hounds raced toward the intruders. Should he call the dogs off?

Telling:

He felt his heart break.

Intimate:

His chest ached as if jackals had savaged his heart.

Telling:

Derek scanned the food court, but he didn't see Ann. He thought she'd stood him up.

Intimate:

Derek scanned the food court. No sign of Ann. Great. She'd stood him up.

Give the action, like scanned, but don't tell the reader his eyes couldn't see.

5. Don't Use Prepositional Phrases to Name Feelings

Don't sneak in "telling" phrases that begin with prepositions, such as: *of*, *with*, and *in* to name a feeling, attitude, or thought.

Examples:

Telling:

Alice gaped at the shimmering light *with* wonder.

Intimate:

Alice gaped at the shimmering light. Where had it come from? Was there a divine reason for its presence? How long would it stay?

Telling:

David stumbled toward his phone. He doubled over *in* agony.

Intimate:

David stumbled toward his phone. Why did he feel so lightheaded? If he could get to his cell, he'd … "Aargh!" The pain. Like someone wringing his intestines. He clutched his abdomen and doubled over.

Telling:

She lounged on the couch and let out a sigh *of* boredom.

Intimate:

She lounged on the couch and gazed at the overhead fan. One cycle. Two cycles. Three. Four. She closed her eyes and sighed.

Telling:

Nancy hurried to the stage *in* great elation.

Intimate:

She'd won! Nancy shot to her feet and sidled past the people in her row. Anthony would be so proud of her achievement. She strode to the stage.

6. Don't Use *Made*, *Caused*, and *Gave* to Tell Reactions or Feelings

These verbs usually lead to telling and explaining what happened. In DPOV, the POVC wouldn't explain to herself what has happened. (For example: Pain *caused* her to cry. Instead: Pain wrenched her stomach. She doubled over, tears coursing her cheeks.).

Examples:

Telling:

Tom tiptoed into Carl's empty bedroom. Suddenly, his alarm clock sounded and made Tom jump. He thought he'd set off the security system. Then he realized it was Carl's alarm clock.

Test it:

In your head, you wouldn't think:

I tiptoe into Carl's empty bedroom. Suddenly, his alarm clock sounds and makes me jump. I think I've set off the security system. I realize it's Carl's alarm clock.

Intimate:

Tom tiptoed into Carl's empty bedroom. Brrring! Brrring! He jumped and spun in every direction. Had he set off the security system? No. Too close. Oh. Carl's alarm clock.

You or your publisher may prefer to replace the sounds with description: *A shrill jangle blared.*

Telling:

Lisa punched his arm and caused him to yelp. That made him mad.

Test it:

In your head, you wouldn't think:

Lisa punches my arm and causes me to yelp. That makes me mad.

Intimate:

Lisa punched his arm. "Ow. That hurt!" Heat traveled up his neck and face. What a shrew. "How would you like me to sock your arm?"

 ACTION

Read your SAMPLE and, using the list below, find where you as the author have stepped into the story. Rewrite these intrusions so emotions, actions, and thoughts issue from the POVC's viewpoint.

- Keep your character's thoughts and actions linear.
- Don't tell that a POVC thought, wondered, realized, decided, wished, hoped, or knew.
- Don't tell or name emotions.
- Don't state that the POVC is using her senses.
- Don't tell feelings using prepositional phrases beginning with *of*, *with*, and *in*.
- Don't use *made*, *caused*, and *gave* when they tell or explain reactions or feelings.

Examples of Getting Inside the Character:

Rick raised the lid on the breadbox. Empty. He yanked open the refrigerator and received a blast of rotten-vegetables odor. The top shelf held a Sippy cup half full of apple juice and an unopened liter of diet orange soda. No milk. Would he and the kids outlive Lily's depression? He grabbed his keys off the counter and headed for the garage.

Chris opened his newspaper. "I think I'll power wash the house tomorrow."

Clare rolled her eyes. Chris still hadn't fixed the dryer. Or taken the unsightly wood at the side of the house to the dump. She'd grow a mustache before he removed his broken-down Harley from her parking space in the garage. So tomorrow, he was going to power wash the house? In her dreams.

Continue to work on reader-character intimacy revisions in your SAMPLE from yesterday and then complete the following segment addressing your POVC's senses.

If Your Hero Doesn't Smell, You May Have A Senseless Story

People use their senses every minute of their day, so your POVC should use all five of his senses in every scene.

Without your POVC smelling scents, tasting flavors, hearing sounds, seeing settings, or touching people and things, he'll seem to live in a vacuum. However, don't dump his use of senses into your scenes. Weave them into the context of the scene's surroundings and actions.

Examples:

Dumped aroma:

"Why didn't you support me when I told the police I was with you?"

"Because I thought they'd say all wives claim their husbands were with them." Was that chocolate she smelled?

"Well, I wish *my* wife had told the truth."

"Should I go back to the police station and give them your alibi?"

Crafted scent:

They sat close in companionable silence. The watermelon scent of Clay's gum complemented the red and orange sunset on a warm summer night. Now, if he'd ask her to watch every sunset with him until death do they part, she'd never run away again.

Crafted taste:

Greg had caught her in a lie. She deserved his arrogant reprimand. How long would she have to swallow the bitter taste of pride?

Patrick took a sip of the lemonade Jill brought as a peace offering. As soon as the sour liquid hit his tongue, his lips puckered. Jill must have forgotten to add sugar. Or … she was declaring war.

Crafted sound:

The doorbell chimes echoed through the empty house. Grant startled and fumbled his flashlight. Why would anyone come down that long driveway to a darkened house that hadn't been occupied in five years? Loud and urgent pounds came on the door. His heart raced as he approached the foyer.

Crafted touch:

Lani hefted one end of the heavy door. The splintered edge drove a sharp sliver into her finger. "Ow." She returned the door to the ground and sucked her finger. Maybe it was time to find some gloves and ask for help.

Crafted sight:

Corrina surveyed the room. So, this would be her space for three months. It would take that long to get it into livable shape. The sheer curtains gave no privacy. Where was the door to the closet? Did Aaron expect her to stare at the boxes on its shelf and hang her dresses on the rusty hangers? She drew open the top dresser drawer. A cockroach skittered along one grimy side.

Remember, don't tell the reader the POVC smelled; show him experiencing an odor. The same applies to the POVC's other senses.

 ACTION

Read your SAMPLE and, using the list below, make sure your POVC uses all five senses in every scene, if possible. Weave his senses into what he's doing or into what is happening around him.

- Scent
- Taste
- Sound
- Touch
- Sight

RESOURCES

Rivet Your Reader with Deep Point of View by Jill Elizabeth Nelson

Where to Add Zing to Your Story

You can add zing to conflict, dialogue, and internal dialogue through simple techniques to boost your reader's interest.

Conflict—Make the Tension Worse

Readers thrive on tension. Create conflict moments in your scenes so deliciously tense that readers worry about the outcome.

A great way to add tension is to write conflict into a scene. Then make it worse. Repeat this until you can't make the conflict any worse. You may rewrite as many as ten times!

Here's an example of the process for the suspense genre, but you can make tension worse in any genre. The example rewrites the conflict five times. I use synopses for conciseness.

Example:

Setup:

Exhausted from her long shift at the hospital, Leah rides a bus to the park-and-ride lot. All she wants is to relax at home with her son, Grayson, and husband, Anton.

First draft:

A man boards the bus at the next stop and plops down beside Leah. She struggles to stay pleasant to the windbag. Then he invites her to dinner. She says she's married. After his bad-tempered reaction, she fears he might follow her home. So, she remains on the bus until he gets off. She's an hour late getting home.

Make it worse:

Forget the windbag. A blonde boards the bus and sits beside Leah. Leah realizes the woman is Dilly Cross, the girl who stole her boyfriend in high school. Dilly opens the conversation, saying Leah looks worn out. Then she asks what has happened in the last fifteen years to make Leah look ten years older than her age. When Leah is speechless, Dilly says she's a psychiatrist at a mental institution and will be glad to help Anton check Leah into a program. Startled, Leah wonders how Dilly knows Anton's name.

Make it worse:

Before Leah can respond, Dilly peers at Leah and asks how Grayson is enjoying third grade at Anderson Elementary School. Leah demands to know how Dilly knows about Grayson. Dilly says her son, Finch, is in Grayson's class. Finch is the boy who has bullied Grayson. Leah confronts Dilly about Finch's bullying. Dilly suggests Leah stop making complaints about Finch at the school office—if Leah knows what's good for Grayson.

Make it worse:

Dilly says she'd hate Grayson to meet with an accident. She adds that Finch sometimes goes berserk. Alarmed, Leah demands to know what Dilly means. Dilly replies the only sure way Grayson won't have an accident is for Leah to supply Dilly with drugs from the hospital where Leah works. Leah realizes Dilly's presence on the bus is no accident.

Make it worse:

Dilly laughs at Leah's stunned expression. "Relax. I don't want drugs. But I'm tired of stealing men from you." Shocked, Leah says she doesn't understand. Dilly says Anton was easy to seduce, but now he doesn't want her anymore. With a wild-eyed gaze, Dilly says, "No one dumps me." Leah begs Dilly to reveal why she's bent on ruining Leah's life. Dilly replies, "Your mother should've never taken Daddy away from my mom and me." Leah claims Dilly is lying. Dilly raises an eyebrow. "Don't worry—darling sister—I'm through taking your men, because as of this afternoon, I've got Grayson. Finch will enjoy his cousin. You'll never find us or see Grayson again. He's mine."

 ACTION

Read your SAMPLE and look for moments of conflict and opportunities to increase the tension. Rewrite conflicts until you've made the reader worry about the outcome. Remember you're not trying to create melodrama but a worse situation within the confines of your story.

That's the end of Day 13. Tomorrow we'll address dialogue and internal dialogue.

Metaphors and Similes in Dialogue and Internal Dialogue

Surprise readers occasionally with a metaphor or simile. Make it relatable to the reader's experience. These literary devices help readers picture people and actions. Make sure the ones you choose are fresh.

A *simile* is a comparison using *like* or *as*. A *metaphor* is a comparison that states an object, concept, or person is something else.

Examples:

Simile: Sarah danced *like* a music-box ballerina. Hadn't the child learned any steps besides spin? Her skinny legs wobbled. Time to close the lid on her performance before her tutu-clad tush ended up on the hardwood floor.

Metaphor: Dancing Sarah was a top-load washing machine set on spin.

ACTION

As you review your SAMPLE to improve dialogue and internal dialogue in the next two subsections, look for opportunities to use metaphors and similes.

DIALOGUE

Dialogue, along with supporting actions, can bring characters' personality alive and show something about their moral fiber. It can move the plot along, supply information in a way more interesting than narration, and break up narration with delightful interludes.

First, let's work through some basic dialogue principles.

Explaining Dialogue—a No-no

Great dialogue needs no added explanation of how the speaker feels. The dialogue should show the character's emotions. However, adding an action beat can help show the character's feelings and let the reader know who's speaking.

Examples:

Emotion explained:

"You've got to be kidding," Jack said in irritation.

Rewrite:

Jack whisked off his glasses and rapped them against the document. "You've got to be kidding."

Emotion explained:

"Oh, Suz. I love, love what you've done. I really do," Liza gushed. (Obvious gushing.)

Rewrite:

Liza clasped her hands to her cheeks. "Oh, Suz. I love, love what you've done. I really do."

Emotion explained:

"I'm not sure ... I know what you're talking about," John said guardedly.

Rewrite:

"I'm not sure"—John took a step backward—"I know what you're talking about."

Sticking to *Said* for Speaker Attributes

Readers need to know who the speaker is for each bit of dialogue. Thinking the reader will understand the dialogue better, writers often use actions for speaker attributes that have nothing to do with speaking. Writer's energy is better spent in writing good dialogue and keeping the speaker attributes simple and invisible, like *said*, or if you must, *asked*.

Examples:

Awkward attribute:

"I've got to wash the floor all over again," Sandi groaned.

It's nearly impossible to groan and speak these words. Try it. If you can groan and speak simultaneously, is the result how you'd want your character to say it?

Rewrite:

"Ugh! Now I've got to wash the floor all over again," Sandi said.

Or

Sandi groaned. "Now I've got to wash the floor all over again."

Awkward attribute:

"I don't think you like me much," Theresa pouted.

People don't pout words; they speak words.

Rewrite:

"I don't think you like me much." Theresa's bottom lip protruded.

Or

"I don't think you like me much," Theresa said.

Dialogue Unique to Each Speaker

If three of your characters are in conversation, the following aspects of each person's dialogue should be so unique that readers would know who's talking without speaker attributes or action beats.

Readers identify characters by

- their word choices,
- the way they put their sentences together,
- how they express under their normal attitude,
- the subjects they pursue, and
- their expressions, grammar, pauses, and interruptions.

Strictly from the dialogue, who is the speaker in each case below, Sandi, her mother, or her husband?

Examples:

"Oh, no! Now I've got to wash the floor all over again."

"Oops. Sorry, babe. Guess wiping my boots on the garage mat wasn't enough, huh.

"I'll make quick work of cleaning up the mud. You two sit outside and enjoy a few minutes rest with each other."

Dialogue Interruptions

Dialogue can have two types of interruptions: one character interrupts another or the speaker interrupts herself. The examples show how to format the interruptions.

Character Interrupts Character:

Karol grabbed her keys. "I think I'll drive over to—"

"You can't. Doug has the car."

Character Interrupts Herself:

"This"—Deanna held up the cream puff—"is art."

Dialogue tips:

- Characters don't always say what they mean. ("Your dress suits you." Not.)
- Often characters use actions to speak for them. (She rolled her eyes.)
- Characters create conflict through what they say. ("What do you mean by that ridiculous comment?")
- Characters speak truth from their perspective, but that doesn't mean they're right. ("Forgiveness doesn't make anything better.")
- Sometimes characters are irked, and they keep the conflict going intentionally. ("Don't turn away from me. We're not done.")
- Characters express their defensiveness through dialogue. ("Well, I didn't hear you say you were ready to leave.")
- Characters may understand the other character's position, but they don't want to give in. ("Even if I could have done better, you had no call to be so rude.")
- Repetitive dialogue mirrors reality, but it bogs down the story. ("I wanted to uh see if you uh wanted to uh go to uh California with me.")
- Keep dialogue concise, making every word count. Don't let characters belabor a point. (See below.)
- Dialogue should include subtext, which is the character's meaning beneath the dialogue. (See below.)

Example of dialogue belaboring a point:

"Miranda's behavior is going to ruin her reputation."

"It's already ruined. Richie broke their date."

"I'm not surprised, the way she acted at Darin's party."

"She should be more careful what she says."

"Yeah. She should be more careful what she does too.

"Miranda's behavior is atrocious sometimes."

"Especially, when she stays out all night and doesn't get any sleep."

Are you sick of the discussion on Miranda's reputation yet? The first two sentences would suffice to convince the reader Miranda's reputation is in trouble.

Example of subtext:

Angie sat next to Paul. "What did you have for lunch?"

Paul turned toward her. "Spaghetti and garlic bread."

"Sounds scrumptious after my small salad. I'm so hungry, I think I'll have a mint. And to show you how nice I am, I'll share one of my mints with you."

"I'm good."

"I've already gotten two out of my purse, so you might as well take one."

Angie isn't hungry or particularly nice, she wants Paul to eat a mint to freshen his breath.

Zingers

Include at least one zinger in every scene. These fresh, unexpected comebacks are guaranteed to enliven your dialogue. Zingers work for any genre.

A dialogue zinger is a

- clever remark skillfully delivered,
- shocking or unexpected observation,
- bold truth, and/or
- dry or humorous comment.

Zingers zing a person in the conversation. The zinger "attacks" the other person's behavior or character in some manner.

Common example:

"I may be drunk, Miss, but in the morning I'll be sober and you will still be ugly." **Zing!** (clever remark skillfully delivered - Winston Churchill)

Other examples:

"You have no intention of marrying me ... and I'm good with that." **Zing!** (shocking or unexpected observation)

(To an adult grandson about a girl.) "Grandson, I love you, but you're an idiot." **Zing!** (bold truth)

Here's an example from my book, *Calculated Risk* (dry or humorous comment). Nick and Cisney are getting ready to drive to his home for Thanksgiving, the trip they wish they'd never agreed to. He's amazed at her two large suitcases for the long weekend. We're in Nick's POV.

Did she think they were staying until next Thanksgiving?

She came around to the back. "What's the matter?"

He opened his trunk and gauged the space.

She stood beside him. "Kind of tight, huh?"

He'd have to stow his carry-on bag and one of her suitcases on the backseat.

"Do you want to take my car?"

"No." He tossed the bag inside the car.

"You're angry."

He walked around her and hefted one suitcase into his trunk. "No. Just amazed."

"No one called to tell me whether Thanksgiving at your home was casual or dressy, so I had to pack for both." Ice capped her words.

"I didn't know your cell took only incoming calls." **Zing!**

It wouldn't have shut her up if Nick had said, "So why didn't you call me?"

Here's a zinger for the suspense genre.

How many times do I have to tell you, I didn't steal this heroine. I bought it."

"Bought it? You just bought yourself a hole in the head." **Zing!**

Suppose the thug had said, "I'm going to shoot you." The statement is the truth but has no punch.

 ACTION

Review dialogue in your SAMPLE. Use the list below to help you look for ways to bring your scenes to life with dialogue.

- Don't explain the speaker's emotions. Write dialogue and action beats that show the speaker's emotions.
- Use the invisible *said* or *asked* or action beats to let the reader know who's talking. Keep the dialogue center stage.
- Give each character a unique dialogue style so characters don't all sound alike.
- Use em dashes (—) when something interrupts the speaker.
- Build conflict through dialogue.
- Show speakers' defensiveness, perspective, and stubbornness through their dialogue.
- Include subtext in dialogue.
- Keep dialogue tight. Temper repetitiveness that mirrors actual dialogue.
- Don't belabor a point in dialogue.
- Include at least one zinger in each scene.
- Look for opportunities to use metaphors and similes.

INTERNAL DIALOGUE

Internal Dialogue (aka direct and indirect thoughts, interior monologue, and inner dialogue) presents the character's thoughts, preferably in deep point of view. It gives the reader information that actions and dialogue can't do as well.

What Internal Dialogue Can Show Better Than Dialogue

Internal dialogue works well for showing the following characteristics.

Emotions

Example:

No matter what Ellen did, he'd never let her know she'd gotten to him. But man, this heart pain made fooling her harder every day.

His internal dialogue shows his struggle with his feelings for Ellen.

Truth

Example:

"That's okay." About as okay as a knife in the back.

The reader learns the truth through internal dialogue that what the other character did or said was not okay.

Hopes

Example:

Mom, Melissa, and Daniel had deserted her one way or another. What now?

A butterfly landed on her muddy shoe. Was it a sign of a brighter tomorrow?

The reader understands the woman still has hope.

Dreams

Example:

Allie studied the woman, her mannerisms, and her clothes. Someday, she'd be that woman. No doubt about it. All she needed was one little break.

Through internal dialogue, the writer reveals Allie's dream for success.

Beliefs

Example:

If only Zena could see how her strong codependent relationship with Mark prevented him from healing. But tell her that? What good would that do? Zena would launch into a monologue about Mark's needs and that she was the only one who could help him.

The reader learns the character's belief about codependent relationships, especially for Zena and Mark.

Humor

Example:

"Wow. Phenomenal." More like phony-menial. How much longer was he going to have to listen to this guy?

The reader receives his real opinion about the conversation through the speaker's internal dialogue wit.

Internal Dialogue Tips

- Give the thoughts of the POVC only.
- Write as if the character is talking to herself.
- Use italics for internal dialogue rarely. Use them to emphasize a short direct thought only, and write the thought in first person. (*I don't think so, bub.*)
- Avoid "thinker" attributes, such as he thought. Just let the character think.
- If the character can speak the thought aloud, put it into dialogue. This often makes dialogue more interesting and prevents internal dialogue from slowing the dialogue's pace.
- Keep internal dialogue concise, making every word count. Don't let the character belabor an issue.
- Repetitive thoughts mirror reality, but they bog down the story.
- Remember the purpose of internal dialogue is to move the plot along or develop characterization.

Example:

Before applying tips:

"I've had enough, Marissa. Do what you want." *It's your life*, Anthony thought as he strode from the room.

Marissa stared at the spot Anthony had vacated. *Do what I want? Do what I want?* He'd never done what she wanted. She remembered the time she wanted to go to the movies, but he didn't want to. What she really wanted was to become his wife. But he'd given no indication of proposing to her. Anthony always did exactly what he wanted to do, like buying a sports car that ruined her hairdo.

He wasn't the only one who'd had enough. *I arranged to teach overseas because I'm tired of waiting.* She wished he'd come to his senses and just ask her to marry him.

After applying tips:

"I've had enough, Marissa. Do what you want. It's your life." Anthony strode from the room.

Marissa stared at the spot Anthony had vacated. Do what she wanted? Well for starters, she wanted to become his wife. But a woman needed a proposal to do that, right?

And how could he say he'd had enough? That was her line. Was he so obtuse he couldn't see she was done waiting, the whole reason she'd decided to teach overseas? If he had a better solution, she'd like to hear it. And it'd better start with him dropping to one knee.

 ACTION

Review internal dialogue in your SAMPLE. Use the list below to help you look for ways to bring your scenes to life in internal dialogue.

- Remove thoughts that don't belong to the POVC.

- If the scene is heavily weighted toward action and dialogue, look for places that short thoughts would help the reader understand the character's emotions or motives.

- Rewrite long italicized direct thoughts as internal dialogue. Write the rare direct thought in first person and italics.

- To write in DPOV, remove thinker attributes.

- If the thought can be said aloud, change it to dialogue.

- Tighten internal dialogue especially when the POVC goes on about the same issue or repeats himself.

- If the internal dialogue doesn't add to the plot or characterization, delete it.

- Look for opportunities to use metaphors and similes in internal dialogue.

Way to go! You've completed Section 2. This concludes the focus on your SAMPLE's scenes. In Section 3, we'll work on the details—words, sentences, and paragraphs.

RESOURCES

From the Inside … Out: Discover … Create … and Publish the Novel in You by Susan May Warren

Techniques of the Selling Writer by Dwight V. Swain

Delight in the Details
Days 15 - 18

Build Story with Words—the Right Ones

Choosing the right words and putting them together efficiently cause the words to disappear and images to arise with every sentence.

The Right Word

Mark Twain said, "The difference between the almost right word and the right word is really a large matter — 'tis the difference between the lightning-bug and the lightning." Like Twain, you will want to give your words the power to create robust images in readers' minds.

Three Quick Steps to Find the Right Word

Step 1:

Read the sentence. Determine whether its job is to stir emotion or simply to keep the reader grounded in what's happening. For the latter, you don't want to bring undue attention to the action. In this case, verbs and nouns that get the job done are sufficient. An action beat that indicates who speaks the adjacent dialogue is often this type of sentence.

> Eric gave Elle the paper.

You don't need to spend much time on such a sentence. However, if the sentence needs to evoke emotion, you do.

Step 2:

Have a thesaurus handy. Select the verbs and nouns in your sentence.

> Noun = paper
>
> Verb = gave

Imagine Eric's emotion. Discern how he feels about Elle and the paper. Be more specific as to what the paper is—a bill, a test paper, or an eviction notice? Now, picture how Eric gives or brings the paper to Elle. Let's look at the first attempts for three cases.

Examples:

> Elle has presented Eric with divorce papers. Eric is incensed.
>
> Noun = paper → document
>
> Verb = gave → shoved

> Eric brings his first book contract to Elle. Eric is elated.
>
> Noun = paper → contract
>
> Verb = gave → waved

> Eric reveals to Elle a biblical document he found in a cave. Eric is awed.
>
> Noun = paper → scroll
>
> Verb = gave → presented

Step 3:

Using your thesaurus, look for a better verb and noun to describe the paper and Eric's action. List a few possibilities. (This action can be done in your head.) Then choose the right one. Even for the no-emotion action beat above, *handed* may be better than *gave*. (Eric handed her the paper.) But you don't want to be overdramatic. The more intense word isn't always the right word. For example, don't use *fiasco* when the situation is a *blunder*.

> **Examples:**
>
> Eric is incensed.
>
> Noun = paper → document → divorce papers → divorce contract → marriage death sentence
>
> Verb = gave → shoved → thrust → threw → flung → hurled
>
> **Eric flung the divorce papers at Elle.**
>
>
> Eric is elated.
>
> Noun = paper → contract → book contract
>
> Verb = gave → waved → flapped
>
> **Eric strode toward Elle, flapping the book contract.**
>
>
> Eric is awed.
>
> Noun = paper → scroll → scroll fragment
>
> Verb = gave → presented → laid → transferred → rested → deposited → slid
>
> **Eric rested the ancient scroll fragment on Elle's upturned palms.**

The Right Fit and Meaning

Besides capturing the emotion of a sentence, nouns and verbs need to fit the characteristics of the subject and the action, respectively. Also, the definition of the word must support your intended meaning.

Examples:

William had listened to enough of her _____. "Excuse me, madam, duty calls me elsewhere."

Choices:

- boring talk
- dribble
- prattle

The definition of *dribble* is a trickle. The writer must have meant *drivel*. One definition of *drivel* is nonsense talk. *Prattle* means foolish talk. *Boring talk, jabber,* or *babble* may work well for the current day, whereas *prattle* may work better for a period in which *madam* and *duty calls me elsewhere* are spoken.

Honey _____ from the cabinet and dripped onto the counter.

Choices:

- ran
- oozed
- spread

Ran is too fast for honey. *Spread* may be what the honey is doing inside the cabinet, but not what it's doing from the cabinet. *Oozed* is the best of these choices.

The following table gives some alternatives for overused words.

Suggestions for Overused Verbs

Overused Verbs	Alternative 1	Alternative 2	Alternative 3
walked	strolled	ambled	strode
ran	dashed	sprinted	jogged
pulled	yanked	dragged	tugged
looked	scanned	examined	stared

Overused Verbs	Alternative 1	Alternative 2	Alternative 3
touched	brushed	tapped	rubbed
reacted	blanched	jolted	sniffled
took	gathered	grabbed	gripped
hit	pummeled	slapped	punched
sat	perched	settled	slumped
lay	reclined	flopped	lounged
left	fled	escaped	deserted

A Singular Noun

If possible, choose the singular of a noun. It's usually stronger than
the plural.

Example:

She turned on her cell. Its light brought mosquitoes to her car window.

Rewrite:

A mosquito fluttered against her car window, determined to reach the glow from
her cell's screen.

Example:

The old man sat on a park bench. He breathed in the summer air. As soon as the
ice cream truck turned the corner, the schoolboys on the swings and jungle gym
sprinted toward it. They lined up at its window, pulling money from their pockets.
If only he could be a schoolboy again and get excited at the approach of an ice
cream truck.

Rewrite:

The old man sat on a park bench. He breathed in the summer air. As soon as the
ice cream truck turned the corner, a red-headed schoolboy jumped off the jungle
gym and raced to the truck's window. He pulled a bill from his pocket, slapped it
on the counter, and reached out his hand. The old man smiled. If only he could
be like that red-headed schoolboy again and get excited at the approach of an ice
cream truck.

 ACTION

Read your SAMPLE, focusing on verbs and nouns. Look for vague
nouns and make them specific—nouns that create images. Search for

weak verbs and replace them with verbs that reflect the paragraph's emotion and intensity level. Conversely, allow the nouns and verbs in sentences you've used in grounding the reader, such as a beat or a transition, to remain subdued. And tone down melodramatic words. Where it works, replace plural nouns with a singular one.

Examples:

Before:

Sounds came from the kitchen.

Kelly turned the sound off on the TV. "Chad, is that you?"

She didn't hear anything, but that didn't mean someone wasn't there.

She looked up at the cabinet where Chad kept his guns. Could she get to the cabinet, take the key from the top, unlock it, and pull out a gun before the person came into the room? No.

Calling for help was the only hope she had. She looked around for her phone. She couldn't find it.

The sounds occurred again. She screamed and screamed.

Better:

A thud came from the kitchen.

Kelly muted the TV. "Chad, is that you?"

Silence.

She swallowed. A dull bump like a sack of sand dropping to the tiles didn't happen without a cause.

She eyed the gun cabinet. Could she stride to the cabinet, locate the key on top, unlock the door, and grab a rifle before the intruder reached the den? No. Calling 911 was her only hope.

She scanned the couch and end table for her cell. Was she sitting on it? She rose.

The thud came again. She clamped her hand over her mouth and scuttled to hide behind the drapes.

Today we'll work on unnecessary words and wordy phrases.

Weasel Words

A weasel sucks the egg from the shell, leaving the shell looking like a whole egg, but it's empty. Weasel words are words that suck the life from adjacent words, which then become less powerful. However, sometimes a weasel word is the right word. Before you cut weasel words from your sentences, consider whether they fit dialogue or the POVC's personality. Also, rewording a sentence is sometimes a better solution than deleting a weasel word.

Examples of weasel words:

Just

I just hate being late.

Just robs half the power of *hate*. Without just, all the emphasis is appropriately on *hate*.

I hate being late.

Just works when used for showing time. *She could tell by his warm coffee mug that he'd just left.* If we remove *just*, it changes the meaning of the sentence.

Very

Disliking her brother was very wrong.

Wrong isn't a vague word. Degrees of *wrong* aren't necessary. *Very* sucks out *wrong's* decisive nature.

Disliking her brother was wrong.

Rather

He took the news rather well.

Similar to *very*, *rather* is unnecessary.

He took the news well.

Some

She spooned some corn into the bowl.

Some works in: *I bought cherries. Won't you have some?* But in the corn example, some is unnecessary. If an amount of corn is important, *some* is too vague.

She spooned corn into the bowl.

She spooned three servings of corn into the bowl.

Immediately

She slapped his face. He immediately grabbed her arm.

If we remove *immediately*, we wouldn't think he did something else before he grabbed her arm. *Immediately*, powers down the action in grabbed.

She slapped his face. He grabbed her arm.

Suddenly

After midnight, the doorbell suddenly chimed. Eva froze.

Suddenly tells us nothing new. It doesn't add fear. The time of night and Eva's reaction shows us the scariness of the passage. Let *chimed* retain its own powerful sound.

After midnight, the doorbell chimed. Eva froze.

Sure

He sure loved her.

Sure drains the love out of *loved*.

> He loved her.

Really

> His sister really deteriorated after Paul moved away.

Deteriorated is already a strong word. *Really* separates the sister from her problem and takes the emphasis off her deterioration.

> His sister deteriorated after Paul moved away.

That

Be careful on this one. *That* often produces clarity. But many times, it adds wordiness. Remove or reword sentences to get rid of unnecessary occurrences of *that*.

> She realized that Randy didn't care that she was ill, and that made it easier to leave him.

Removing unnecessary occurrences of *that*:

> She realized Randy didn't care she was ill, and that made it easier to leave him.

(If we're in her POV, *She realized* is also unnecessary.)

Or reword the sentence:

> Randy's indifference to her illness made leaving him easier.

Almost

Sometimes almost works but often it's unnecessary.

Works:

> From the ladder, she could almost reach the apple.

Here, the apple was an inch out of reach.

Unnecessary:

> She was almost interested.

Either you're interested or you're not.

Rewrite:

> He'd piqued her interest.

Started to/began to

These phrases are only necessary when a character starts or begins to do something and then stops doing the action.

Works:

> She started to cross the room. Alex grabbed her arm and spun her around.

Unnecessary:

> On the other side of the room, Ken talked to Ron. She started to walk across the room and admired how handsome Ken looked in his tux.

Rewrite:

> On the other side of the room, Ken talked to Ron. She walked across the room and admired how handsome Ken looked in his tux.

Up/down (as used with words such as stood, started, sat)

> When she arrived, he stood up.

The reader knows when someone stands the direction is up.

> When she arrived, he stood.

> He started up the car.

When start means to get something going, up is unnecessary.

> He started the car.

When she heard the bad news, she sat down on the chaise.

When someone sits from a standing position, the reader knows he's moving downward.

When she heard the bad news, she sat on the chaise.

Adverbs ending in –ly

An adverb ending in –ly works when it gives needed information while moving the story along. It works when no verb can replace an adverb-verb combination, and when showing the action would slow the story. Also, an -ly adverb works when a character would use the word in dialogue. However, many adverbs ending in –ly are unnecessary words that slow the pace.

Many adverb-verb combinations can be replaced with a strong verb.

walked confidently → strutted

hit repeatedly → rapped or hammered

ran quickly → sprinted

Consider the adverbs in the following paragraph:

Jason planted his hands *firmly* on top of the gate, swung his legs over *gracefully*, hit the ground *lightly*, and took off after Lily. He couldn't lose her this time. Lily *really* needed to hear what Dad had said about her before he *quietly* died. Maybe she'd *finally* stop running and return to the family.

Solutions for the –ly adverbs:

Firmly - Change *planted his hands firmly* to *gripped*.

Gracefully - Delete it; it slows the pace and plays down the urgency of Jason's problem.

Lightly - Delete it or rewrite Jason's landing more realistically.

Really - Delete it; it sucks the punch from *needed*.

Quietly - Delete it; it inserts a speed bump in the flow. How Dad dies is not important at this moment.

Finally - Could delete it, but it supports the idea that Lily runs every time she sees family members. Using *finally* is much shorter than going on about her constant fleeing.

Rewrite:

> Jason gripped the top of the gate, swung his legs over, hit the ground, and took off after Lily. He couldn't lose her this time. Lily needed to hear what Dad had said about her before he died. Maybe she'd *finally* stop running and return to the family.

ACTION

On your SAMPLE, perform a search-and-find for each weasel word in the checklist below. Decide whether the word is necessary. Cut or rewrite unnecessary occurrences. Remember, sometimes a weasel word is the right word in dialogue as long as it doesn't become repetitive. Also, keep the word *that* when it provides clarity.

- ☐ Just
- ☐ Very
- ☐ Rather
- ☐ Some
- ☐ Immediately
- ☐ Suddenly
- ☐ Sure
- ☐ Really
- ☐ That
- ☐ Almost
- ☐ Started/began
- ☐ Up/down (as used with words, such as stood, started, sat)
- ☐ ly (to find adverbs ending in ly)

Prepositional Phrases

Prepositional phrases communicate relative position, time, possession, purpose, or method. Some prepositions are unnecessary, and some are misused. The good news is that sometimes you can and should end sentences with prepositions. If a sentence sounds wordy or you need to reread it, eliminating or rewording prepositional phrases will help.

Examples:

Unnecessary:

- He went inside *of* the house. → He went inside the house. (position)
- Where had he gone *to*? → Where had he gone? (position)

Misused:

- They rode to the ranch with horses. → They rode to the ranch on horses. (method)
- He'd been driving since three hours. → He'd been driving for three hours. (time)

End with a preposition:

Sometimes ending with a preposition feels right—and it is.

- From where did you get that ice cream? → Where did you get that ice cream from? (position)
- On what did you put the flowers? → What did you put the flowers on? (position)

Overusing Preposition Of

The preposition *of* often introduces unnecessary phrases. You can eliminate wordiness, create smoother reading, and locate other problems by reviewing how you've used *of*. Observe how rewriting *of*-phrases in the following examples reduces wordiness.

Examples:

Amount and Number:

- cleaned every trace of dirt from the ball → scrubbed the ball clean
- stared for a couple of beats → stared for a moment
- have a couple of clients in Florida → have clients in Florida (or have two clients in Florida)
- from all of her comments → from her comments
- done in plenty of time to → done in time to
- a lot of gossip about her → much gossip about her
- chose one of the less expensive restaurants → chose a less expensive restaurant

Directional:

- rolled two feet past the other side of the cup → rolled two feet past the cup
- started at the top of her head and flowed to her toes → flowed from her head to her toes
- nodded in the direction of → nodded toward
- chairs rested on either side of the couch → chairs flanked the couch
- stared at him from the other side of the table → stared at him across the table

"Of The"

- read sections of the newspaper → read newspaper sections
- curbed their talk in the presence of the lady → curbed their talk in the lady's presence
- from the window of the dining room → from the dining room window
- adjusted the angle of the racquet → adjusted the racquet's angle

 ACTION

Perform a search-and-find for the preposition *of* in your SAMPLE. Eliminate or rewrite wordy phrases containing *of*. Sometimes, an *of*-phrase is a better option, especially when multiple possessive words arise. (The church's organist was Alice's mother's friend. → The church organist was the friend of Alice's mother.)

Wordiness

Phrases Beginning with *Made*

Avoid phrases beginning with *made* (*make*).

Examples:
- made a decision → decided
- made use of → used
- made a correction → corrected
- made great improvement → improved

 ACTION

Perform a search-and-find on your SAMPLE for the word *make* or *made*, depending on your story's verb tense. If *made* heads a wordy phrase, replace it with one word that says the same thing.

Wordy Phrases

Rewrite wordy phrases.

Examples:
- due to the fact that → because
- was unable to → couldn't
- in need of an estimation → needed to estimate
- in the area of dealing with → in dealing with
- under the circumstances in which → when
- how to respond to her fears → how to face her fears

Passive Constructions

The word *by* is a clue that your sentence may be in passive voice. When someone or something is being acted upon by someone or something else, the construction is passive opposed to active.

Examples:

- Her hope was ignited by him. → He ignited her hope.
- Her dress was drenched by the rain. → The rain drenched her dress.

Keep sentences active, unless you have a reason to tone down the pace or feeling. For example, if a character doesn't want to sound accusatory, she might say, "I was hurt by what you did," instead of "You hurt me."

 ACTION

Perform a search-and-find on the word *by* in your SAMPLE. If it produces a passive sentence, rewrite the sentence in active voice, unless a speaker is toning down a reprimand.

Vague Beginnings

Avoid *it was*, *there was*, and *there were*.

Examples:

- It was her belief that he'd erred in his ruling. → She believed he'd erred in his ruling.
- There was much to do before bedtime. → She had much to do before bedtime.
- There was still time to make it right. → He had time to make it right.

 ACTION

Perform a search-and-find on the word *there* in your SAMPLE. If it's part of *there was*, *there is*, or *there were*, rewrite the sentence if possible. Do the same for *it was* and *it is*.

Inflated Words

Inflated words are words that seem like they've been pumped up with formality.

Examples:

- had an impact on → affected
- facilitated → helped
- was cognizant of → knew

Strings of Nouns

Stringing nouns together causes confusion. Clarity trumps sentence length.

Examples:

- She used the inpatient inquiry method therapy. → She asked probing questions.
- The women's technology assistance center was closed. → The center where women could ask questions about their electronic devices was closed.

Special Cases

Multiple-Word Exclamations

Your character exclaims multiple words as if it's a single word with no pauses. No commas are used.

Examples:

- "Oh boy."
- "Oh no."
- "Oh yeah."
- "No no no!"

Utterances

Your character uses utterances. Here are common ones. Some have alternate spellings. Use these sparingly.

Examples:

- Yes → uh-huh, yeah, yep

- No → uh-uh, nope
- Confused → huh? eh?
- All right → OK, okay
- Amazed → Ooh, wow, whoa
- Bored or boring → ho-hum; yadda, yadda, yadda
- Clearing throat → ahem, harrumph
- Disgusted → bah, ew, sheesh, phooey, tsk, ugh, yuck, gak, aargh, harrumph
- Dumb → duh, doh
- Exuberant → wahoo, whee, yay, yee-haw, yippee
- Enlightened → ah, ah-ha
- Catch off guard → gotcha, ha!
- Get attention → ahem, ahoy, psst, yoo-hoo
- Like it → mmm, yum
- Pained → aargh, ouch, ow, yeow, oomph
- Proud → ta-da, shazam
- Puzzled → hmm, huh
- Relieved → whew, phew
- Sneeze → ah-choo, atchoo
- Surprised → oh, whoa, ooh, uh-oh
- Touched → Aw
- Wrong → oops, whoops, uh-oh, oopsy-daisy
- Hesitation → ah, er, eh, erm, uh, um

The Word *Which*

Here's how to write the word *which* in various cases. Watch for the presence and omission of commas.

Examples:
- He didn't know which way to go. (direction)
- After her blunder, her cheeks flamed, which added to her embarrassment. (added information)

- He always gushed over how pretty I was. Which was a pack of lies. (emphasis)
- He always gushed over how pretty I was—which was a pack of lies. (emphasis)
- He always gushed over how pretty I was, which was a pack of lies. (added information)
- Our family reunions were always the sort at which my cousin tortured me with snide comments. (prepositional phrase)
- I was stuck in a situation for which I had no solution. (prepositional phrase)

 ACTION

Perform a search-and-find on the word *which*. Either eliminate commas when it's used in a prepositional phrase or for direction, or include commas if it introduces additional information.

Multiple Adjectives

Sometimes having multiple adjacent adjectives that are very different can stop the reader so he can form an image from all the adjectives. If you have more than one adjective, the best practice is to choose the most defining one and delete the other(s). If you think all are equally good, use the deleted adjectives in other sentences in the paragraph.

Examples:

Two adjectives

A flirty, red-lipped secretary approached Sam. How was he going to convince Marcia that the woman was only an acquaintance from the third floor?

One adjective

A flirty secretary approached Sam. How was he going to convince Marcia that the red-lipped woman was only an acquaintance from the third floor?

Note how the reader must picture a flirty woman's actions in the first sentence while also picturing her red lips. In the next sentence, the reader can now picture her red lips separately from picturing how she swishes her hips.

Three adjectives

Patsy detested when a telephone caller asked for a charity donation. She'd ask the next pushy, gum-chewing, fast-talking caller to give twenty dollars to each of the charities she supported.

The reader may pause to picture how the caller chews gum and talks fast. The word *pushy* best describes what Patsy detests. *Fast-talking* could be used in a different spot in the paragraph.

One adjective

Marcie detested pushy telephone callers who asked for a charity donation. She'd ask the next fast-talking caller to give twenty dollars to each charity she supported.

On rare occasions, you may need to use more than one adjective. Here's a suggested hierarchy that shows which adjective should be first in the series.

Adjective Hierarchy Guidelines

- Quantity – exact or general number
- Opinion/Observation (tasty)
- Size
- Temperature
- Age
- Shape
- Color
- Origin (French)
- Material (brass)
- Purpose – -ing-words (sleeping bag)

Examples:

1. Three elderly French priests
2. Beautiful auburn hair
3. A Teflon frying pan
4. Oval green eyes

In the previous examples, the order of the adjectives produces phrases that sound good and make sense. Separating commas weren't used because the last adjective and the noun are seen as a unit, for example, auburn hair is described as beautiful.

If *and* cannot be placed between the adjectives, no comma is used. We wouldn't write beautiful and auburn hair, so no comma. Also, if reversing the order of the adjectives makes no sense, no comma is used. We wouldn't write auburn, beautiful hair or auburn and beautiful hair. So, again, no commas.

Example:

The small, blue bowling ball was perfect for my determined, active son.

Let's test the commas for all the adjectives in this last example.

The small and blue and bowling ball was perfect for my determined and active son.

And works between *small* and *blue* and between *determined* and *active* (both opinion/observation adjectives) but fails to work between *blue* and *bowling*. So, the commas are correct in the original version. Let's see if the sentence makes sense if we reverse the adjectives separated by commas.

The blue and small bowling ball was perfect for my active and determined son.

The blue, small bowling ball was perfect for my active, determined son.

The sentences still make sense, but *blue and small* might sound better if the order suggested in the hierarchy guidelines is used. See the original sentence above.

ACTION

Peruse your SAMPLE for the items in the checklist below and fix any problems you find.

- ☐ Unnecessary or misused prepositions other than *of*
- ☐ Wordy phrases
- ☐ Inflated words
- ☐ String of nouns
- ☐ Multiple-word exclamations
- ☐ Utterances
- ☐ Multiple adjectives

RESOURCES

Flip Dictionary: For When You Know What You Want to Say But Can't Think of the Word by Barbara Ann Kipfer, Ph.D.

Compose Palatable Paragraphs

*Readers should never have to wade through tedious paragraphs
or need to read paragraphs more than once.*

Today, your only activity is to read this chapter about the common problems that occur in paragraphs and the suggested solutions. You will edit your SAMPLE on Day 18 with the help of a checklist.

Start a New Paragraph

Paragraphs in fiction are less structured than those in nonfiction. In fiction, writers go by one rule and several guidelines. We'll work through a partial scene to show the rule and guidelines in starting new paragraphs. The guideline numbers in parentheses at the end of each paragraph indicate the reason for a new paragraph.

Rule: Always start a new paragraph when you switch speakers in dialogue.

Guidelines: Start a new paragraph when

1. a new character reacts, does something, or thinks something;

2. time moves forward or backward;

3. as in movies, the camera angle changes;

4. a new idea arises;

5. information isn't closely related to information in the current paragraph and needs to be distanced;

6. a new event happens;

7. the setting changes;

8. the reader needs a break from a long paragraph;

9. a change in emphasis or tone occurs;

10. description of one thing ends, and something else is described; or

11. a special effect is needed to add humor or drama.

Example: (Corresponding Rule and/or the Guideline numbers are noted after these sentences.)

"How do you suggest we handle this one?" Jack said. (Rule, 1)

Mandy's eyebrows shot up. "Me? You're the expert." (1)

Jack turned his back on Mandy and strode to the fence. He needed to think. When had he dealt with a similar situation? The field grass on the other side of the fence swayed in the wind. That was it. He'd swayed the general in the Haitian op four years ago. (2)

The pompous Haitian general had detained and questioned Jack's men for over an hour. Jack had needed to free his men before the general became suspicious of what they'd been doing ashore in the middle of the night. He'd come up with a plan that had stretched his acting skills. (8)

He'd burst into the compound pretending to be furious with his men for sneaking off the ship to find an open bar. Then he'd played to the general's ego and told him he was right to question his disobedient men. The puffed-up general reprimanded Jack's suddenly repentant sailors and released the men. (2)

If Mandy and his men were caught today, would that tactic work on the warlord? But Mandy wasn't one of his men. (5)

His orders were to obtain the intel. How was he going to do that with Santiago's men combing the area for his unit? (1, 3)

"So, what've you come up with?" Mandy approached him, twirling a dandelion between her thumb and forefinger. "Remember, Santiago knows me." (1, 4)

Jack exhaled a heavy breath. He couldn't take Mandy out of the op. She was the only one who knew what to look for inside Santiago's files. (4, 10)

Mandy's mother had told him Mandy had a photographic memory. If he could get Mandy inside to scan the pertinent files in Santiago's underground cave, he'd have the information he needed. (6, 11)

Rat-tat-tat! (1)

Jack jerked his head up. The machine gun fire was close. Santiago's men were busy routing out their own people, looking for the Americans. Jack needed to get Mandy to his unit. (1)

Mandy grabbed his arm. "How much time do we have before Santiago's soldiers reach us?" (Rule)

"Come on. We gotta put distance between his goons and us." (3, 6)

They sprinted to their gear, swept it up, and headed for the village. (7, 6)

On the other side of the village where he'd left his men, the place was empty. Not even a local villager peering out a window. Without his men, he and Mandy needed a hiding place. (9)

Now.

Vary the First Words of Paragraphs

Another paragraph problem is beginning several paragraphs in a row with the same word.

Example:

Andy led the boys to the boathouse and told them to collect all the oars stored in the boxes along the back wall. Hollering, they raced to be first to reach the boxes. He shook his head. They should save their energy to handle the river rapids.

He climbed the hill to the house to collect the lunches Marcia had packed for them. The bulging sacks full of sandwiches, fruit, and snacks should give the boys the vitality they needed to row for the next four hours.

He piled the lunches into the wheelbarrow from under the house and wheeled the unstable vehicle down the hill. He should be saving his own strength.

He assigned three boys to transfer the lunch sacks to the five canoes when he reached the dock.

Notice three paragraphs in a row start with the word *he*. To the reader, this will sound repetitive. A few easy changes improve the sound and flow of the paragraph.

Andy led the boys to the boathouse and told them to collect all the oars stored in the boxes along the back wall. Hollering, they raced to be first to reach the boxes. He shook his head. They should save their energy to handle the river rapids.

The sun baked his head and back as he climbed the hill to collect the lunches Marcia had packed for them at the house. He should be saving his own strength.

He piled the lunches into the wheelbarrow from under the house. The bulging sacks full of sandwiches, fruit, and snacks should give the boys the vitality they needed to row for the next four hours.

When he reached the dock wheeling the unstable vehicle, he assigned three boys to transfer the lunch sacks to the five canoes.

Add Specifics and Vary Sentence Structures

To produce interesting paragraphs, add specifics and fix monotonous sentence length, form, and style.

Example:

Her car stopped. She tried to start it again. The engine wouldn't start. Lissa fearfully evaluated her situation. She was miles from a service station. Kenzie slept in the backseat. At least she wasn't frightened.

Lissa wished Colby was with them. He was a sizable man. No one would mess with him.

She turned on her cell. It had no service.

Suddenly, lights reflected from the mirror.

Rewrite:

The Honda Pilot's engine sputtered and died. Her heart racing, Lissa wrenched the steering wheel hard right, and the SUV coasted off the remote road, miles from help. She shot her gaze to the rearview mirror and then twisted her shoulders right and left. All locks were engaged, and no attacker lurked outside in the night.

The low-gas light flickered. The Pilot was out of gas? Impossible. The gas gauge registered full two hours ago. She turned the key. The starter grated like a garbage disposal grinding a peach stone.

The car was not going to start.

She released the seat belt, threaded her hand between the front seats, and brushed her index finger against sleeping Kenzie's bare foot. Her daughter's lips parted and closed in a soft snore. Hopefully, her toddler would miss the entire frightening incident. Unlike herself.

Lissa turned to the front, wrestled her phone from her handbag, and thumbed her cell to life. No service. She dropped her head back against the headrest. What now?

If only her two-hundred-pound Colby sat in the passenger seat. Kenzie's daddy could scare away a zombie. But a jet flew him to the other side of the US. Lissa bit her lips together, willing tears to stay put.

Headlights reflected off the rearview mirror. She punched the all-lock button. Twice.

Backload Paragraphs

Your goal is to entice your reader to read the next paragraph. The worst way for your reader to leave each paragraph is reading a vague word, such as *his, it, with, there,* or *was.* These words leave the reader with no gist of the paragraph's meaning or how he should feel as he starts the next paragraph. A paragraph backloaded with an evocative word excites readers subconsciously to move forward in the story.

Examples:

> Carrie clamped her mouth shut, unwilling to rile a man who carried a rifle under his arm and a hunting knife strapped to his leg.

This version leaves the reader with the man's leg. If the sentence was about his wounded appendage, *leg* could be appropriate. But the paragraph is about Carrie's fear of the man's weapons.

> Carrie clamped her mouth shut, unwilling to rile a man toting a rifle and a hunting knife with a twelve-inch blade.

A knife is an up-close weapon and scarier than a rifle that can wound from a great distance. Add a twelve-inch blade and the reader leaves the sentence understanding Carrie's fear.

Here's another example:

> He was still dead no matter how long she stared at him.

The reader departs the paragraph with the vague pronoun *him,* which tells him nothing about this short paragraph.

> No matter how long she stared at him, he was still dead.

In the second version, *dead* gives the reader the finality of the situation. The reader will want to know what the character is going to do next.

As often as possible, end each sentence in a paragraph with a power word that hints at the meaning of the sentence. This next example is from my romance, *Calculated Risk.* Suppose I had written:

> She splayed her arms over her paper-covered desk and knocked her head on it. The fault was Jason's. Space was what Jason wanted? Right. What he needed was freedom to date that woman with the small waist.

The words *it*, *Jason's*, *wanted*, and *waist* don't link the reader to Cisney's life, how she feels, or anything about Jason. Here's the paragraph taken from the book.

She splayed her arms over her paper-covered desk and knocked her head on the piles. This was all Jason's fault. Jason needed space? Right. What he needed was freedom to date that woman with a waist the size of his muscular neck.

- *Piles* points to Cisney's disordered desk and life.
- *Fault* shows how she feels about Jason in her predicament.
- *Space* points to Jason's lame excuse.
- *Muscular neck* leaves the reader with the feeling of a powerful person hurting vulnerable Cisney. Because the reader knows Nick is on his way to Cisney's office, hopefully the reader will want to know what Nick is like in contrast.

Show, Don't Tell

Telling a character's feelings or what happened is faster, but showing these brings the reader into the story. Showing is worth the extra work and words.

Example:

When Maud spoke harshly to the child, Jack looked at Maud with disdain.

Questions might run through the reader's mind. What did Maud say to the child? What does Jack's disdain look like? The reader is uncertain what happened and whether Jack was irritated or incensed. Without more information, the reader doesn't know how to react emotionally to the scene.

Rewrite:

Maud jabbed her finger at Jillie's desk. "Get all your disappointing papers together. Now!"

Jack drew himself up to his full height. He arched his eyebrow, curled his upper lip, and glared at Maud. Was she getting his message? His dog had more tact than the shrew.

See how showing helps the reader picture what really went on outside and inside Jack. The reader may feel worse for the child, knowing what was said, yet she can cheer how Jack responded, picturing his disdain through what he did and thought.

Example:

Bob felt sad his granddaughter didn't want to visit him anymore.

What does sad mean to Bob?

Rewrite:

Bob ran his fingers over Nell's sweet face in her school photo. Why'd she have to grow up and prefer her friends to riding the tractor with Grandpa? He pulled off his glasses and wiped away the mist that had formed on the lenses.

We sense Bob's loneliness and his love for Nell, through his viewing her photo and thinking of their past camaraderie, which brings him to tears.

Example:

The man was old.

Rewrite:

The wind beat the man's thinning hair about his face, and silver wisps caught in the crow's feet edging his rheumy eyes.

Showing brings the old man to life.

Example:

The stranger scared the boy.

Rewrite:

As the stranger approached, the boy's eyes widened, and he hid his face in the folds of his mother's skirt.

Showing is important, but sometimes telling gets the job done the best way. If thoughts, feelings, or actions are less important than something else in the paragraph, don't slow the pace by showing. First let's look at an example of telling.

Example:

Brent ignored me and looked at Cassie. "You can't go with me. That's final."

Cassie watched Brent stride across the parking lot, then rotated toward me. "What's his problem?"

Cassie watched is telling. Let's see what showing would do to the paragraph.

Rewrite:

Brent ignored me and looked at Cassie. "You can't go with me. That's final."

Cassie's gaze trailed Brent's retreat, her eyes narrowed, and her lips pressed together. When he climbed into his car, she rotated toward me. "What's his problem?"

Here *watched* is sufficient, because showing Cassie's gaze and expression slows the pace to arrive at her snappy statement. But suppose Cassie said, "What did I do wrong?" Then, showing her emotion would make sense.

Rewrite:

Cassie's gaze trailed Brent's retreat, her eyes narrowed, and her lips pressed together. When he climbed into his car, she rotated toward me. "What did I do wrong?"

Too Much: Reduce

Don't burden readers with excessive details, repetition, and overexplaining. These problems bog down the story, and readers feel like they're plowing through a thesis.

Excessive Details

When you include excessive details, readers skim paragraphs, looking for substance and the plot.

Example:

Her family members would arrive in an hour. Time to set the table.

Evelyn held one end of the tablecloth, ejected the rest of the cloth over the table, and let it settle onto the tabletop. She gave the corners and ends a few tugs to get it centered. She carried china plates to the table and distributed them, making sure each plate rim was two finger-widths from the edge of the table. She went back to the kitchen for the salad plates and dispersed them. She stood on stool steps and brought down the box of silverware from the cabinet over the refrigerator. She wiped each fork, knife, spoon, butter knife, salad fork, and large serving spoon with a soft cloth to remove any smudges. Once they gleamed, she set each utensil in its proper place. She also wiped the crystal goblets with the cloth, then set the glasses at the tips of the knives. She folded the peach napkins into birds of paradise and laid them on the plates. She finally placed the seating placards at the top of the plates.

We'll identify more problems in the above paragraphs later, but the above 170-word paragraph describing Evelyn setting the table doesn't advance the plot and tells little about Evelyn, except that she's exacting. Let's see how we can write a tighter paragraph that tells something about Evelyn and the plot.

Rewrite:

Her family members would arrive in an hour. Time to set the table.

Evelyn arranged Mama's china and Grandma's crystal goblets on the linen tablecloth, placing the plate rims two finger-widths from the table edges and the crystal goblets a thumb's width above the tip of the silver knives she'd buffed for smudges. She topped each plate with a peach napkin folded into a bird of paradise, which she'd learned how to create from cousin Mavis before their falling out. As she centered placards at the tops of the plates, she sniggered. How unfortunate that no placard read Mavis. Evelyn smiled. Would Aunt Bea ask why her daughter was missing from the family dinner?

The second paragraph, sixty-seven words less than the first, shows that Evelyn is exacting, values the family heirlooms, and enjoys excluding her cousin from the dinner. We're unsure what will happen when Aunt Bea realizes her daughter is missing.

So, keep details concise and meaningful to the story or to the characters' personalities.

Example:

Jane reached with her right hand, grabbed the coffee mug, and brought it to her lips. "What makes you think he's the murderer?"

Avoid detailing humdrum body movements when one or two words can do the job.

Rewrite:

Jane sipped her coffee. "What makes you think he's the murderer?"

Repetitions

Go back to Evelyn's overly detailed table-setting example. Notice that eight sentences start with *she*. The rewritten paragraph has one.

Use synonyms and rewrite sentences to cut down on repeated words.

Example:

Garrett enjoyed the light wind as he sipped his sweet tea. Within seconds, the wind picked up and blew his cloth napkin off the table. When he stood to retrieve his runaway cloth napkin, a robust bout of wind blew his toupee up from the back of his head, then slapped it over his eyes.

The above paragraph uses *wind* three times and *blew* and *cloth napkin* twice. Here's a rewrite replacing the repeated words with synonyms.

Rewrite:

Garrett enjoyed the breeze as he sipped his sweet tea. Within seconds, the wind picked up and blew his cloth napkin off the table. When he stood to retrieve the runaway serviette, a robust gust rocketed his toupee up from the back of his head, then slapped it over his eyes.

Serviette may not fit your audience or tone. In this case, in the second mention of the *cloth napkin*, use only *napkin* to make it less noticeable.

> Within seconds, the wind picked up and blew his cloth napkin off the table. When he stood to retrieve the runaway napkin, ...

Using Marcie's problem with telephone callers asking for donations in Chapter 9, this next example is riddled with repetitions.

Example:

> She detested and disliked pushy telephone callers asking for money for charities. They always asked her to find it in her heart to give twenty smackers. She gave thousands to charities that were important too. She couldn't fix every problem in the world. She'd ask the next fast-talking caller to give twenty smackers to each of the charities she gave to.

Notice *She* opened four sentences. Three forms of *ask* and four forms of *give* were used. The rarely used word, *smackers*, sticks out and feels repetitive when used only twice. The verbs *detested* and *disliked* are close in meaning. Only one is necessary. In the rewrite below, Marcie purposely engineers the play on *fix* and *fixed*; therefore, these words wouldn't be considered repetitive.

Rewrite:

> Marcie detested pushy callers hounding her for money for good causes. They always asked her to find it in her heart to give twenty dollars. Weren't the organizations she donated thousands to equally important? How much of the world could she fix on her fixed income? She'd suggest the next fast-talking caller contribute twenty bucks to each of her preferred charities.

Overexplaining

When you explain an action or what was said in another way, you risk offending readers. Readers aren't dumb. Resist the urge to explain (RUE).

Example:

> She hunched over her plate. She ate spoonful after spoonful of the beef stew. She was hungry.

The reader will understand she is hungry without the author adding the explanation.

Rewrite:

She hunched over her plate and shoveled beef stew into her mouth.

Sometimes the overexplaining is less obvious, but it's still unnecessary.

Example:

Tim leaped over the hedge, taking a running start, springing from the ground, and sailing over its top leaves.

Leaped (or *leapt*) is a strong verb that readers can picture.

Rewrite:

Tim leaped over the hedge.

However, if Tim had been worrying how he was going to get over the hedge, an explanation may show how he accomplished the feat.

Tim took a running start, sprang from the ground, and sailed over the hedge, his soles grazing its top leaves.

Too Awkward: Change

Nonlinear Actions (Also see **Remain in the Now**, in Chapter 7.)

The story should unfold in the order actions and events happen so the reader's mind isn't constantly shifting gears.

Example:

Paul pulled out his Glock after he jumped aboard the barge. He feared more than one man was on the other side of the stacked crates. Before he peeked around the corner of a large wooden box, he said a prayer.

This paragraph is nonlinear and telling. Let's put the actions in the order they occurred and make the paragraph more interesting by showing his fear.

Rewrite:

Paul jumped aboard the barge and pulled out his Glock. What were the odds that more than one man was on the other side of the stacked wooden boxes? High. Would they be armed? His knees shook, and a bead of sweat plunked onto his hand. He ran his sleeve over his face. *Lord, protect me.* His weapon extended, he edged forward and peeked around the corner of a large crate.

Out-of-order actions also arise when a character reacts before a stimulus occurs.

Example:

Carrie wrenched the door open, gasped, scuttled backward, and fell. Jack's body filled the doorway, his knife glinting in his fist.

Rather than create suspense for the reader, the reader's thoughts shift backward to the reactions, and then he says, "Oh, that's why she gasped, scuttled backward, and fell."

Rewrite:

Carrie wrenched the door open. Jack's body filled the doorway, his knife glinting in his fist. She gasped, scuttled backward, and fell.

Example:

Sally hurried to stash Jack's letter under the mattress when she heard Max's approaching footsteps.

Placing the reaction first stops the forward motion of the story while the reader wonders why Sally hides the letter. Below, let's see how to keep the reader moving forward in the plot *and* add suspense.

Rewrite:

Downstairs, the front door closed. Max was home. Sally's heart thudded and her hands shook. The stationary bent and wouldn't go inside the envelope. Max's footsteps grew louder, approaching the staircase. If he caught her with Jack's missive, he'd leave her, destitute. She stuffed the letter and envelope into her slacks pocket. A white corner protruded. Oh no. She wrangled the papers free as the loose step on the staircase groaned. Where could she hide the condemning message? Her gaze darted around the bedroom. Sally lifted the bed comforter, and as the doorknob turned, she stashed the papers under the mattress.

Confusing Sentences and Paragraphs

When phrases are in the wrong place, readers reread paragraphs, trying to figure out who did what when.

Example:

Greg had forgotten to tell Ginger he'd seen three wild turkeys playing golf the other day.

Wow. Turkeys playing golf! Let's fix the sentence.

Rewrite:

Greg had forgotten to tell Ginger while playing golf the other day he'd seen three wild turkeys.

Oops. Now Alice played golf with Greg? Let's try again.

Greg had forgotten to tell Ginger that while he played golf the other day, he'd seen three wild turkeys.

When several pieces of information are thrown into a paragraph, it can become convoluted and confusing.

Example:

By reaching across the cement wall, Ziggy grabbed the malfunctioning Tiki torch Mom had lodged there with the hand she burned in last night's fire lighting up the area with it to expose thieves climbing over it, snagging her sweater in the process.

Huh? Let's rewrite, rearrange, and break up the long sentence into two sentences.

Rewrite:

Ziggy eyed the malfunctioning Tiki torch Mom had lodged outside the wall to expose thieves entering the yard. She reached the hand she'd burned in last night's fire across the cement wall and grabbed the torch, snagging her sweater in the process.

Vague Sentences and Paragraphs

Vague words such as *it*, *that*, *her*, *them*, and *him* can refer to more than one thing or person.

Example:

Sissy gaped. McKenzie had told Jace every detail about her past. McKenzie's big mouth would someday get her in trouble. That hurt her now.

First, is the paragraph talking about McKenzie's or Sissy's past? Will McKenzie's big mouth get McKenzie or Sissy in trouble? What hurt? McKenzie's gossip, McKenzie's big mouth, or somebody getting in trouble? And who was hurt?

Let's see if the following rewrite straightens everything out.

Rewrite:

Sissy gaped. McKenzie had told Jace every detail about Sissy's past. McKenzie's big mouth would someday get McKenzie in trouble. But now, her deceitful gossip had destroyed Sissy's chances to marry Jace.

Clarity trumps reducing the repetition of names. I could use *her* in the third sentence because McKenzie is the subject of the previous sentence, and the reader knows McKenzie gossiped.

Usually, you can catch these convoluted paragraphs after you've let them sit awhile.

Separation of Subject and Verb

Avoid cramming too much into a sentence and distancing the subject from the verb.

Example:

Kelly, though usually competent and strong, but realizing this was a horrific situation and help would only come from her and no one else, not even Chris, *felt* scared and upset.

Rewrite:

Kelly was usually competent and strong, but this was a horrific situation. Now, no one, not even Chris, could help her. Her whole body trembled. What was she going to do?

Impossible Actions

Often the use of participial phrases (using -ing verbs as adjectives) creates impossible simultaneous actions.

Example:

Setting her suitcase on the floor, she walked away.

This says she's setting her suitcase on the floor while walking away.

Rewrite:

She set the suitcase on the floor and walked away.

And can mean one idea or action is chronologically sequential to another. Here's another example of impossible simultaneous actions.

Example:

Pulling on his pants, he extracted coins from his pockets and counted the change.

Rewrite:

He pulled on his pants, extracted coins from his pockets, and counted the change.

Italics

Italics used to emphasize words, to indicate thoughts, or to format long online chats are awkward to read. Use italics for the rare emphasis of a word or for direct thoughts in which a character speaks to herself, to God, or to someone else. One option to write online chats or texts is to change the chat or text content to another easy-to-read font.

Examples:

Emphasis:

I guess you *could* say that but you'd be *wrong*, because *I'm* the one who'll get the job.

Rewrite:

I guess you could say that but you'd be wrong, because *I'm* the one who'll get the job. (Or removing all italics would work fine.)

Thoughts:

Will hit a home run. Damien slammed the bat against the dirt. *Will got all the cheers. How could such a skinny guy send the ball over the fence?* Will dropped the bat and pounded his thigh. *Why can't you hit like Will?*

All thoughts are written in italics, including Damien speaking directly to himself in present tense.

Rewrite:

Will hit a home run. Damien slammed the bat against the dirt. Will got all the cheers. How could such a skinny guy send the ball over the fence? Will dropped the bat and pounded his thigh. *Why can't you hit like Will?*

All thoughts are written without italics, except Damien's direct thought to himself in present tense.

Rewrite :

Will hit a home run. Damien slammed the bat against the dirt. Will got all the cheers. How could such a skinny guy send the ball over the fence? Will dropped the bat and pounded his thigh. Why couldn't he hit like Will?

All thoughts are written without italics and Damien's direct thought converted into a third person, past tense thought like his other thoughts. The Rewrite examples are easier to read.

More examples of direct thoughts:

Jason wasn't breathing. Brian started CPR. *Lord, please bring Jason back.*

Erin opened Mom's jewelry box. Surely, Amy had returned Mom's diamond earrings by now. Erin searched all the velvet-covered sections. The earrings were missing. *Way to go, Erin. You're in big trouble.*

Online chat:

Deanna: *Have I got news for you guys.*

Rod: *News or gossip.*

Blair: *I'm up for some good gossip.*

Deanna: *Lucy made an F on her history exam. Her dad grounded her for a month, but she sneaks out every night and meets some guy at the library. I bet Lucy is going to ditch Paul.*

Blair: *Tiffany is my best friend. She's crazy about Paul. I'll let her know she'll soon have a chance with Paul so she can be first in line to flirt with Paul.*

Rod: *Deanna, did you ever consider how harmful spreading gossip is?*

Deanna: *I believe people should know the truth.*

Rod: *So do I. I'm the guy helping Lucy with her history homework and test preparation at the library. Both Lucy's parents and Paul know of the arrangement and applaud her efforts to succeed in history class.*

Rewrite:

Deanna: Have I got news for you guys.

Rod: News or gossip.

Blair: I'm up for some good gossip.

Deanna: Lucy made an F on her history exam. Her dad grounded her for a month, but she sneaks out every night and meets some guy at the library. I bet Lucy is going to ditch Paul.

Blair: Tiffany is my best friend. She's crazy about Paul. I'll let her know she'll soon have a chance with Paul so she can be first in line to flirt with Paul.

Rod: Deanna, did you ever consider how harmful spreading gossip is?

Deanna: I believe people should know the truth.

Rod: So do I. I'm the guy helping Lucy with her history homework and test preparation at the library. Both Lucy's parents and Paul know of the arrangement and applaud her efforts to succeed in history class.

Progressive Tense

Usually, the progressive tense (*was* [or *is*] + an *-ing verb*) is unnecessary. This tense should be used only when the simple past (or present) tense doesn't work. The progressive tense is cumbersome to read. Let's determine which progressive tense occurrences are necessary in the next example and which can be replaced with past tense.

Example:

When Lisa called Brandon, he was eating dinner. As he told her how his mother was doing after her accident, Lisa was remembering how they had eaten dinner together every night in their college days. She was realizing how much she missed their conversations.

We can evaluate what doesn't work by changing all the verbs to past tense.

Test it:

When Lisa called Brandon, he ate dinner. As he told her how his mother did after her accident, Lisa remembered how they had eaten dinner together every night in their college days. She realized how much she missed their conversations.

Ate in the first sentence, and *did* in the second fail our test. Past tense works for *remembered* and *realized*.

Rewrite:

When Lisa called Brandon, he was eating dinner. As he told her how his mother was doing after her accident, Lisa remembered how they had eaten dinner together every night in their college days. She realized how much she missed their conversations.

Too Odd: Cut

Darlings

Most writers have heard British journalist, critic, and novelist Sir Arthur Quiller-Couch's saying, "Murder your darlings." He's referring to phrases or whole passages that the writer thinks are clever and interesting, but they only draw attention to themselves and interrupt the plot's progress. They can sound forced or as if the piece or the writer is saying, "Look at me." You must approach your "darlings" as an impartial editor. Then you'll see them for what they are and axe them.

Examples:

Graham walked on the treadmill by the gym windows. Callie's whole body sagged as if a hundred-pound weight sat on her heart. Should she skip today's session? Their presence together in the same gym wasn't working out.

Callie, a bodybuilder, would think of the heaviness of a hundred-pound weight on her heart when referring to her lovesickness. But the pun about being in the same gym together not "working out" is inappropriate for the seriousness of her hurt feelings. The "darling" needs to go.

> "You'll find Victoria frequenting only high-class, posh, and trendy places. I tell you, the woman is an ambiance chaser."

The pun might be something the speaker would say; therefore, the pun could stay.

Clichés

Unless a character would think or speak clichés, avoid them or rewrite them to make them fresh. Using clichés is lazy writing. Most readers don't want to read others' overused phrases; they want you to entertain them with new ways to look at life.

Examples:

> Grayson strummed his guitar to beat the band. Gail was on cloud nine. Maybe after the gig he'd pay her attention and treat her like his main squeeze. She was pretty sure his bark was worse than his bite.

Try making an old cliché fresh.

> Mom's appraising gaze suggested she had more bones that needed picking.

Examples of Overused Phrases

A word to the wise	Every fiber of my being	Look down your nose on
As luck would have it	Fishing for a compliment	Make the best of it
Avoid it like the plague	Few and far between	Manicured lawn
Blow off steam	If walls could talk	Off the top of my head
Burning question	In his element	On a roll
Cold shoulder	Keep an eye on	Sigh of relief
Crystal clear	Know the ropes	Take the tiger by the tail
Caught in the crossfire	Lick your wounds	Thick as thieves
Dead as a doornail	Like a kid in a candy store	When push comes to shove

DAY 18

Review and Revise

 ACTION

Using the information from the above sections and the checklist below to help you, read your SAMPLE and correct paragraph problems.

- ☐ Start new paragraphs appropriately.
- ☐ Vary the first words of paragraphs.
- ☐ Vary sentence length and style.
- ☐ Backload paragraphs (and sentences if possible).
- ☐ Show versus tell.
- ☐ Remove excessive details.
- ☐ Reduce repetitions.
- ☐ Delete explanations of actions and what characters say.
- ☐ Keep subject and verb close in a sentence.
- ☐ Make actions linear.
- ☐ Rewrite confusing or vague sentences.
- ☐ Rewrite sentences that have characters performing impossible actions.
- ☐ Limit italics.
- ☐ Change unnecessary progressive tense uses to simple past (or present) tense.
- ☐ Murder your darlings.
- ☐ Rewrite to remove or freshen clichés.

Bravo! You've completed Section 3 covering word, sentence, and paragraph details. Next, is your opportunity to revise all the scenes beyond your SAMPLE.

RESOURCES

Self-Editing for Fiction Writers: How to Edit Yourself into Print by Renni Browne and Dave King

The Rest of the Story
Days 19 - 30

End Your Story Well to Sell

If you don't backload a satisfying ending to your story, readers may not buy your next book.

In this chapter, we'll look at the tips for a satisfying ending scene(s). When I say ending scene, I don't mean an epilogue.

Tips for a Satisfying Ending

Don't Rush the Ending

The reader will feel like the author wrapped up everything quickly to meet a deadline.

Example:

Let's go back to the *Love Comes Softly* movie example. Spring arrives, and Marty has reconciled her grief and doesn't want to go back East, where she has no one. She hopes Clark loves her as much as she's grown to love him and Missie. In a note she sticks inside his Bible, she writes, "I don't want to go. Ask me to stay."

Suppose Clark finds Marty's note that same day. And suppose he rushes inside the house and declares his love. The end.

Viewers would have missed the final conflict and experiencing how much Marty and Clark suffer for their "integrity" in their commitments. Marty will not stay unless Clark loves her, and he must tell her so. Though legally married, she can't live with him and Missie any longer. Clark sticks to his promise he made the previous fall, that if Marty wants to leave on the wagon train in the spring he will pay for her fare without asking any questions. Viewers also would miss gentle Clark racing to the already moving wagon train yelling her name, finding her, and then giving her the reason for her to stay. Finally, viewers would miss Missie seeing Marty descend from a buckboard with baby Aaron, and for the first time, utter "Mama."

The story is about so much more than the romance; it's about love. Taking the viewer to that realization is worth the work.

Don't End in a Flurry of Conflicts and High Emotions

Cutting off the story when actions and emotions are intense is like characters sprinting to a cliff with bad men in pursuit and the reader turns the page to find "The End."

Example:

Suppose the *Love Comes Softly* story ends right after Clark has his emotional talk with God and finds the note. He has the "oh no" feeling, rushes to sad Missie, and tells her to stay while he goes after Marty. He gallops away on his horse. The end.

Viewers and readers need to come down from the emotional frenzy and witness what the characters feel and do when they're in their more normal state. Their normal state might be joy and the promise of lasting love as in *Love Comes Softly*. In a legal thriller, after a highly emotional court drama and verdict play out, a short scene occurring on the next day might follow. Over breakfast in a diner, the defending lawyer shares with the released defendant how at the last moment he obtained the one piece of evidence that saved the defendant's life.

Resolve Subplots

Unless your book is part of a series, resolve all subplots. Often a series will leave one subplot open to be continued in the next book. Readers of a book series accept an open subplot, but the main plot needs to be resolved.

No subplot should distract readers from the main plot's resolution. And don't draw out resolutions of subplots. Although the reader has earned a rest period in the ending, she doesn't desire a fall-asleep period.

Example:

Consider the subplot in which Marty comes to faith in God. It's resolved in the first half of Act 3. After the barn catches on fire, she prays for Clark's safety, but still doesn't understand why God would let the barn burn down. Clark takes her to his bench overlooking a beautiful valley that he calls his church. He explains that God has always answered his prayers. He likens his care for Missie to God's watchfulness.

Marty wants to stay there awhile alone with God. Having that scene at the end would have distracted watchers from the resolution of the love plot. The faith subplot's resolution needed to come first, before Marty could love the whole man who is Clark. Because Marty's faith journey is a subplot, it needed to be wrapped up satisfactorily by the end, whether she comes to believe in God or not.

Show How Your Protagonist Is a Wiser, More Competent Person

The main character may not achieve the goal he hoped for, but he should be able to do something he couldn't do in the beginning. If he hasn't grown in some way, even if it's to accept that he won't accomplish his goal, readers will feel the time they've spent with him through conflicts and disasters has accomplished nothing. That's not satisfying.

Example:

In the beginning, the only reason Marty is in the West is that she loves her husband, Aaron. She prefers the East and tries to bring a part of it with her by hauling all her books. But near the end, Marty, now a competent prairie woman, is in the women's wagon heading east, because she thinks Clark doesn't love her.

A woman expresses she's glad to be leaving this godforsaken part of the country. Marty says she wouldn't call it godforsaken. The woman complains about the horrible hailstorms. Marty counters with the beautiful sunsets and rich soil. The woman declares a woman must be either crazy or in love to want to stay out West. Marty turns away.

Marty had found a home, friends, and a good way of life in the West, and she wanted to stay—if Clark had loved her. *Love Comes Softly's* ending shows that the story is more than a story about romance and love; it's also about Marty finding where she belongs—finding home.

Make the Ending Unpredictable, Plausible, and Memorable

Although your ending must be plausible and must deliver what readers expect from the genre, give the reader an ending they can't predict. For example, romance readers expect the hero and heroine to get together in the end. This is predictable. But how they finally get together can be something the reader doesn't expect. For example, the reader expects the couple to have it all, but for the hero to choose love, he sacrifices his desire to return to his homeland. For genres other than romance, keep the reader guessing whether the protagonist will succeed or fail at getting what she wants right up to the final moments. Work on your last page until it leaves the reader with something that's memorable and resonates.

Example:

For *Love Comes Softly*, I expected Clark to bring Marty and baby Aaron home from the wagon train. I accepted that the horse Clark races off on is now pulling a borrowed or rented buckboard when they approach the house. I expected Missie to be happy and run into the arms of the woman she calls Marty and has gradually accepted as an encouraging, loving woman. But what I didn't expect and will always remember with tingles is how Missie breathes out in a whisper, "Mama," before she runs into Marty's arms. The story ends quickly after this.

If Your Ending Isn't a Happy One

If your ending isn't a happy one, the reader must at least feel satisfied. Perhaps the protagonist chooses to do something courageous that harms him, but it's best for those he loves. In fact, your ending may be more interesting if it contains a win and a loss.

Example:

Love Comes Softly closes with a happy ending, but suppose the author had a different theme in mind. Suppose Janette Oke wanted to show how difficult life is in the West. In this new scenario, Aaron's brother, Daniel, lives back East. Marty has fondly mentioned Daniel several times. Suppose Clark is killed in the barn fire nearer the end of Act 3. Marty and Missie grieve. Then Daniel shows up to bring Marty home. He has loved her since he and Aaron first met her. The reader sees where this new twist could go. The end.

Create More Than One Ending

Try different endings and see which gives the best emotional satisfaction or introduces a "gotcha." Make sure a twist is believable, though.

Example:

Suppose, near the end, Marty and the settlers think Clark died in the barn fire and wolves carried off his body, because no sign of his body is found in the charred barn. Then Clark shows up a week later. Clark's motive is to make Marty see how much she loves him. This wouldn't be a satisfying ending because not-really-dying is a clichéd gimmick and Clark's action is hurtful and out of character.

Include the Title or Theme

If your story has a strong theme or a title that represents the theme well, including the theme or title may work in your story's wrap-up. But if either feels plunked in or cheesy, neither is right for your ending.

Example:

The words *love comes softly* show up naturally in the beginning of Act 3 when Sarah answers Marty's question about how Sarah can love her husband so intensely now, when their marriage vows were based on survival. Sarah explains that sometimes love comes softly. This is a better place for Sarah to speak the title than at the end when, besides love, the story focuses on romance and a place to call home.

 ACTION

Reread your last chapter, especially the last scene. Ask yourself the following questions. For those you answer *no* to, work on your ending until you can answer yes to all the questions.

- Have you brought closure to each subplot, except one for a sequel? ☐ yes ☐ no
- Have you avoided wrapping up the ending too quickly? ☐ yes ☐ no
- Have you prevented subplots from competing with the main plot during the ending? ☐ yes ☐ no
- Have your characters come down from frenzied actions to allow readers to reflect on the theme, a revelation, or a memorable moment? ☐ yes ☐ no
- Does the ending have an unpredictable element? ☐ yes ☐ no
- If your ending isn't a happy one, is it at least satisfying, i.e., the hero can do something that he couldn't do at the beginning? ☐ yes ☐ no
- Is your story one whose ending would be more powerful with a loss and a win, and you've done this? ☐ yes ☐ no
- If your story ends in a twist, is it plausible? ☐ yes ☐ no
- If appropriate, does your ending pull in the theme in some way that makes your ending memorable? ☐ yes ☐ no

RESOURCES

Plot & Structure: Techniques and Exercises for Crafting a Plot That Grips Readers from Start to Finish by James Scott Bell

Read, Review, and Revise—
Edit Pages Beyond Your SAMPLE

With your better understanding of the areas where your writing is weak, you're ready to edit each scene beyond your SAMPLE.

 to

In this chapter, you'll customize the checklist below to your needs and finish editing your book.

Customize the Checklist According to Your Needs

 ACTION

Carefully read the following checklist and tick each box that accompanies items you've identified as areas you need to focus on as you edit the remainder of your manuscript. Note: the best answer is yes for these questions.

Your Focus		Comprehensive Lists of Editing Tasks	Chapter
☐	1.	Are there three reasons for the scene to exist? Is at least one an essential reason?	5
☐	2.	Does the type of scene (action, reflection, or combo) work best at this point?	5
☐	3.	In an action scene, is the character's overall story or scene goal clear?	5
☐	4.	In an action scene, does meaningful, worsening conflict occur?	5/8
☐	5.	Does a reflection or combination scene follow an action scene?	5
☐	6.	In reflection moments, does a dilemma confront the character?	5
☐	7.	In reflection moments, does the character make a decision?	5
☐	8.	Have you avoided introducing too many new characters?	5
☐	9.	Have you used a fresh scene plot instead of an overused plot?	5
☐	10.	Does the scene open mid-action and grab the reader?	5
☐	11.	Is the reader grounded in Who, Where, When, Mood, and whose POV?	5
☐	12.	Is setting revealed through what the POVC reacts to, sees, hears, and does?	5
☐	13.	Are flashbacks necessary?	5
☐	14.	Can flashback information be gradually fed into the story?	5
☐	15.	Are actions, thoughts, and dialogue believable? Are they true to archetypes?	5/8
☐	16.	Is backstory fed into the scene?	2
☐	17.	Is the scene told from only one POVC's thoughts?	5
☐	18.	Are transitions clear and smooth?	5

☐	19.	Does the scene end with a hook that entices the reader to turn the page?	5
☐	20.	Has the protagonist remained likeable in dialogue and actions?	2
☐	21.	Are walk-on characters given brief but interesting characterization?	2
☐	22.	Is the scene's pace neither sluggish nor too fast?	4
☐	23.	Are humorous moments humorous?	4
☐	24.	Has a suspense element been set up or inserted? Or could one?	6
☐	25.	Are characters' reactions realistic and not melodramatic?	6
☐	26.	Are all POVC's actions and thoughts linear and remain in the now?	7/10
☐	27.	Have you as the author resisted intruding in the scene?	7
☐	28.	Have you shown emotions, instead of naming or telling them?	7
☐	29.	Do you show instead of tell the reader the character is using his senses?	7
☐	30.	Have you avoided *made*, *caused*, or *gave* to tell reactions or feelings?	7
☐	31.	Has the POVC used all five of his senses without dumping them in?	7
☐	32.	Is a metaphor or simile included in dialogue or internal dialogue for interest?	8
☐	33.	Have you avoided speaker attributions that explain the dialogue?	8
☐	34.	Are speaker attributions possible? Could *said*, *asked*, or a beat work?	8
☐	35.	Are the dialogue style and word usage unique for each character?	8
☐	36.	Have you limited word repetitions that mirror real conversation?	8
☐	37.	Is there interesting subtext beneath the dialogue?	8

☐	38.	Is dialogue concise, and does every word count?	8
☐	39.	Have you avoided characters belaboring a subject in dialogue?	8
☐	40.	Is at least one dialogue zinger included?	8
☐	41.	Does internal dialogue show emotions, truths, hopes, dreams, beliefs, and humor?	8
☐	42.	Does internal dialogue sound as if the character is talking to herself?	8
☐	43.	Are italics added only to *rare* emphasized words and first-person direct thoughts?	8,10
☐	44.	Have you left off unnecessary "thinker" attributes?	8
☐	45.	Have you turned POVC's thoughts into dialogue where it works?	8
☐	46.	Is internal dialogue concise, and does every word count?	8
☐	47.	Have you avoided the POVC belaboring a subject in internal dialogue?	8
☐	48.	Does internal dialogue have a few repetitions that mirror real life?	8
☐	49.	Does the internal dialogue move the plot along or develop characterization?	8
☐	50.	Are strong verbs and nouns used?	9
☐	51.	Is the count of overused words low?	9
☐	52.	Have you used a singular noun instead of its plural when you can?	9
☐	53.	Do you use weasel words sparingly?	9
☐	54.	Are wordy prepositional phrases and ones with the word *of* rare?	9
☐	55.	Have you reworded wordy phrases, especially starting with *made*?	9
☐	56.	Have you avoided writing passive constructions?	9

☐	57.	Do sentences starting with vague words like *it* or *there* seldom show up?	9
☐	58.	Do you avoid inflated words or strings of nouns?	9
☐	59.	Is the word *which* used correctly?	9
☐	60.	Have you avoided multiple adjectives and replaced them with the best one?	9
☐	61.	Are new paragraphs started in the right place?	10
☐	62.	Are paragraph sentence lengths and structures varied?	10
☐	63.	Are paragraphs backloaded with meaningful words?	10
☐	64.	Have you shown, and avoided telling, except where the pace needs picking up?	10
☐	65.	Are paragraphs free of excessive details?	10
☐	66.	Are paragraphs and their neighbors without repetitions of the same words?	10
☐	67.	Have you avoided unnecessary explanations of actions or dialogue?	10
☐	68.	Do actions and events unfold in the order they occur – in a linear manner?	7,10
☐	69.	Is it easy to understand who did what in every paragraph?	10
☐	70.	Do sentences keep the subject fairly close to the verb?	10
☐	71.	Do you avoid participial phrases that cause impossible simultaneous actions?	10
☐	72.	When the past tense works, do you use it instead of the progressive tense?	10
☐	73.	Have you left out "clever" phrases that draw undue attention and need to be cut?	10
☐	74.	Have you used freshened clichés or refrained from using clichés?	10

Read, Review and Revise the Remainder of Your Manuscript

 ACTION

For the next eleven days, armed with your personalized checklist, revise the remaining scenes of your manuscript.

Now, your tailored fiction manuscript is ready to move forward. It's up to you whether you send it to Beta readers or a professional editor, query agents and editors, or self-publish the book.

If you're interested in traditional publishing, I recommend that you attend a writers' conference that offers appointments with agents and editors. These appointments allow you to pitch your book to acquisition professionals. If you're not traditionally published yet, most acquisitions editors will require that you have a clean, completed manuscript. You will. Congratulations!

RESOURCES

Proofreading Secrets of Best-Selling Authors by Kathy Ide

AFTERWORD
My Writing Journey

Over the years while I worked full time, I wrote many partial manuscripts. Then, in my budding faith walk, I wrote short stories to explain to myself what I'd heard or read in the Bible or Bible studies. I self-published two books of these contemporary Christian short stories.

I think because I came armed with the two books of short stories and a completed historical romance manuscript, an agent took a chance on me and signed me early on. Acquisition editors rejected that romance. One editor said the writing was not "stand out."

I found critique partners, entered contests for the judges' feedback, attended conferences, and wrote three inspirational romantic suspense novels. The rejections got better. All editors liked my ideas, but my writing needed improvement. However, editors now invited me to submit other projects.

One day, I identified one obstacle that kept me from getting a contract. Writing inspirational romantic suspense required my attention on three elements (spiritual, romance, and suspense). I was always weak in one of the three areas. So, I let go of the suspense element and wrote inspirational romances to see if that solved the problem. It did.

I had almost finished my fifth book, a contemporary inspirational romance, when I attended a popular agent's workshop. He said it took four completed manuscripts to learn to write, and the fifth one usually was published. That was true for me. A traditional publisher contracted my contemporary inspirational romance, *Calculated Risk*.

Around that time, I wanted to research and learn as much as I could about the writing craft. I switched my blog's focus from creativity to sharing what I learned regarding the craft. After two years of publishing weekly posts mostly on writing and marketing books, two industry professionals told me I should publish a book on writing based on my blog posts.

I contracted two more romances, and then I thought I was ready to write a book on writing to help first-time book writers, those who were having a hard time selling their manuscripts, and those who self-published but had low ratings. So, I presented a proposal to one of the two professionals, and her publisher contracted this book.

As of this writing, my second romance, *Gift of the Magpie*, is out, and my third, *The Putting Green Whisperer*, released in September 2018. Also, five other published authors invited me to write a novella for a Valentine's Day 2018 collection. *The Invisible Woman in a Red Dress* was born. I'm working on story for the 2019 Valentine's Day collection. I mention my books so you can see that perseverance pays off. But I hope the work you've done with *Tailor Your Fiction Manuscript in 30 Days* will help you publish successfully before your fifth manuscript. I think it will.

About the Author

Zoe M. McCarthy was an actuary in her first career, but she always held a passion to create stories. Determined to learn the route to publication, she joined a critique group and attended writers' conferences, picking up and studying presenters' books on writing.

When Zoe's first contemporary romance contracted, her research on publishing and marketing convinced her she needed to start a blog and post regularly. Because her analytical side gives Zoe a keen interest in the mechanics and methodologies of good writing, a how-to blog on writing appealed to her. In 2012 she began her blog.

After Zoe had published over one hundred fifty blog posts, an agent and a publishing house editor suggested she write a book based on her blog. The idea interested Zoe, and she attended a workshop on the dos and don'ts for turning blog posts into a book. She wanted to share more than the information she'd accumulated. She desired to help writers who had manuscripts but didn't know how to get them ready for publication, writers whose manuscripts received rejections, writers whose self-published novels received poor reviews, and writers who wanted to write the stories on their hearts but needed help to put them to paper. *Tailor Your Fiction Manuscript in 30 Days* was born.

Zoe still attends writing workshops at popular Christian writers' conferences, subscribes to *Writer's Digest*, and explores online writing articles to improve her writing and her blog posts. Zoe's weekly posts share what she's learned and often include examples of how she incorporated skills and techniques into her own writing.

In addition to her instructional blog, Zoe has taught workshops at libraries, writer groups, and the Virginia chapter of American Christian Fiction Writers' Conferences.

Her husband, John, partners with Zoe on the nonwriting tasks in her publishing career. They live on a hill in the Virginia Blue Ridge Mountains. Zoe and John enjoy exploring mountains and valleys, canoeing the New River, or spending time at their cabin on a lake. They have two sons, two daughters-in-love, and six grandchildren.

Zoe writes contemporary Christian romances involving tenderness and humor. Believing opposites distract, Zoe creates heroes and heroines who learn to embrace their differences. She is the author of *Good Breaks*, *The Putting Green Whisperer*, *The Invisible Woman in a Red Dress*, *Gift of the Magpie*, and *Calculated Risk*. Connect with Zoe at zoemmccarthy.com .

CPSIA information can be obtained
at www.ICGtesting.com
Printed in the USA
FFHW020126100119
50119517-54993FF